Tired, Hungry,
and Kinda Faithful

Tired, Hungry, *and* Kinda Faithful

Where Exhaustion and Exile Meet God

Peyton Garland

RESOURCE *Publications* · Eugene, Oregon

TIRED, HUNGRY, AND KINDA FAITHFUL
Where Exhaustion and Exile Meet God

Resource Publications
An Imprint of Wipf and Stock Publishers
199 W. 8th Ave., Suite 3
Eugene, OR 97401

www.wipfandstock.com

PAPERBACK ISBN: 978-1-6667-9723-7
HARDCOVER ISBN: 978-1-6667-9722-0
EBOOK ISBN: 978-1-6667-9721-3

JUNE 17, 2022 4:01 PM

To my grandmother, Bonnie:
Each book I write will always be for you.
To Josh, my confidant and anchor:
Thank you for believing in me.

Contents

Acknowledgements | ix

Introduction | 1

1   Location, Location, Location | 4

2   The Pricklier Side of Things | 16

3   Wall of Wounds | 24

4   Hay and Healing | 34

5   Goodness Remains | 41

6   An Avenue for Peace | 51

7   Steady Assurance | 61

8   Forged and True | 70

9   Purpose in Ash | 77

10   Chains for Joy | 87

11   Because of Scars | 95

12   Jehovah Nissi | 106

13   Little, Tiny Miracles | 114

14   A Watchtower | 122

15   The Path Home | 131

Final Thoughts | 140

Bibliography | 143

Acknowledgements

To Jehovah Nissi, I give you my eternal devotion. And though my devotion falters amid sin, thank you for sustaining me.

Josh, the father of my dog children, you are the steady wisdom leading our little family. Thank you for being my biggest cheerleader throughout this project.

To Kelly and Phil, had you two not raised me in God's love, I'm unsure where my soul would be today. I owe you my gratitude always.

Olivia, your strength and compassion are the inspiration that gives this book wings. I pray you fly far above this world's fleeting glory and always feel heaven's warmth.

To Bonnie, I'll forever feel your spirit as I write God's truth. Your quiet faith speaks volumes.

Mary, my editor, I count you a true champion of my words and journey. Thank you for your humble dedication to this book.

To all who have reminded me of God's faithfulness, this–my testament of the Lord's light and love in the hardest seasons–is for you.

Introduction

IF YOU ARE READING these words, you, my dear friend, are a survivor. Whether you have discovered these pages in a second-hand bookstore or a friend thought you should give these words a whirl, this paper and ink find you with purpose. The purpose of a survivor.

You weathered the unknown of 2020, the hostility and division of 2021, and no matter which year in the aftermath you have found this story, I am placing a gold medal around your neck. Right here, right now. Why? Because you made it. And in today's world, surrounded by too much noise and too little kindness, making it to the other side is always worth celebrating.

However, this does not, and will not, neglect the tough season you have walked through—or are trudging through now. In war, most survivors return home hollow, scarred, damaged, unpacking ratty, muddied uniforms but stowing away nightmares no one need know about. Most Olympic gold medalists put in years of blood, sweat, and tears to make their way onto the podium, claiming a global athletic spotlight for as little as five minutes. Yet, they carry the grandeur for a lifetime. Getting to the other side of hard things, whether gut-wrenching or glorious, has never come without a price.

This uphill journey makes me think of God's people, the children of Israel. They wandered through the wilderness for forty years, making mistakes, learning lessons, and repeating their mistakes. They lived true days of glory yet adopted a frugal faith, their ungrateful perception of mercy dwindled to only dull, expected monotony. They grew anxious amid their parched surroundings, a dastardly combination of sin and fear wilting their hopes. Meanwhile, in between each near-constant blunder, they turned back to God, over and over again.

Some days, the Israelites were halfway in but halfway out. Committed yet wary.

Other days, they were halfway out but halfway in. Wary yet committed.

They unpacked the powerful faith God gave them, then crammed Satan's lies into their hearts.

They lost sight of perseverance yet persevered long enough to reach the land God promised them generations before.

Some days, doubt had the upper hand, and on other days, hope burned brighter.

In all this wandering, this back and forth amid frivolous doubts and a faith breaking the surface, I think of myself. I can't deny my modern parallel to their lukewarm journey, which calls me to ponder if others, perhaps you, can relate to the children of Israel, or even me. Is there a chance your life is hollow and damaged by the one vice that seems unshakeable? Or perhaps you haven't healed from the blood, sweat, and tears of showing up for the good fight. My heart fervently believes some of you have made it to the Promised Land, and yet, you're tired, hungry, and feeling as if someone exaggerated the taste of milk and honey. This flowing finish line was said to taste sweeter and run deeper through the soul.

But something is damming your joy. In short, your faith in God lives in a glass half empty. Often, when faith cannot keep up with our feelings, we remain stalwart to the latter. We surrender to fleeting emotions surrounding our circumstances until we discover they have forced us one step forward but two steps backward. Then, we have no other choice but to crawl back to faith, allowing it to pick up our slack.

Maybe you think God should be kinder, more gracious, more accepting, in these times. Or perhaps all you want is one tiny answer to one tiny prayer, frustration growing alongside impatience as you challenge God's faithfulness to you, a servant who has been faithful the whole time. After all, a good God should supply good things, especially to his children.

I get it. That is why this book, more like a compilation of empathetic letters, is for you. This book is for me too, a constant return to seasons of my life where the spiritual realm seemed riveting and roaring (whether good or bad, I often had no clue in the moment). Such is the beauty of a mysterious faith.

As Christians, we hear Jeremiah 29:11 on repeat. "For I know the plans I have for you," we mutter. "Plans to give you a hope and future." Yup, yup, we got it. We have undoubtedly seen this monogrammed on a purse or tattooed on someone's wrist ten times over. But Jeremiah 29:14, just a few verses later, blatantly says that God drove the children of Israel into exile. It reads, "'I will be found by you,' declares the Lord, 'and will bring you back from captivity. I will gather you from all the nations and places where I have banished you,' declares the Lord, 'and will bring you back to the place from which *I carried you into exile*'" (emphasis added).

Seems ironic, possibly barbaric, nothing like the character of our God, right? Why would a good God drive his children into a land lacking all resources necessary for survival?

So his goodness could be their sole pursuit. So his love could carry them home. So when they returned home healed, they could truly sing hallelujah over a season God used to bring reason to bloodshed and brokenness.

Amid such mysterious yet marvelous truth, I firmly believe that your season had, has, and will have purpose. That the broken pieces of your spirit are meant to be healed. Your cup destined to overflow with milk and honey, the sweetest, purest kind.

So, whether you're in the middle of surviving, looking in the rearview mirror wondering why tragedy happened, or peeping through covered eyes in fear of the future, I pray these words offer not only peace but purpose.

Take one day at a time, one chapter at a time, as we discover meaning in the hard times, as we find lush life in the most unexpected places.

Let's see what happens when exhaustion and exile meet God.

1

Location, Location, Location

✂

A GEORGIA PEACH BORN and raised, all I knew were skyscraper pine trees, mosquitoes and their breeding creeks, and wild daisies. Boy, I loved picking bushels of those white-petaled, flimsy flowers by the quiet, lazy Hogansville highway. On a successful sunny day, I would peruse the storm pit's latest collection of dust and memories, create a ruckus in the bug-stricken bird-bath, and skip back home with less than ten pesky bug bites running swollen trails up and down the back of my wiry legs. Land was lush, and grass was always green, but it was water that made small-town life seem bigger. Water was a way of life and a means of life.

Bored in the summer at seven years old? I got ya' covered, friend. Us popsicle-sticky southern girls would haul a dirty tarp from behind the nearest dad's rusted shed and steal the blue dish detergent from the closest mom's kitchen sink. Next thing you know, we were slipping and sliding under an arch of hose water, ignoring the belly scrapes from jagged rocks we forgot to chuck away before laying out the tarp. You didn't have to send invites for such aquatic activities. In fact, shirtless boys and shoeless girls would come out of the woodworks, all over the neighborhood, and steal their spot in the slip-n-slide line.

Want to be popular in high school? Even better. Hang on for your life like a bull-riding cowgirl as your friend's favorite uncle zigs and zags a 2004 pontoon boat across greenish water, doing everything to fling you off your tube halfway across West Point Lake. If you make it more than eight seconds, congratulations. You are likely next year's homecoming queen.

Water holds memories for me, lots of sure, steady ones. Better yet, water contains a portal to my escape from harsher realities. When I needed to forget 9/11 drug Dad hours from home, Mom would pack my sister and me in a grungy green van and drive us to his naval station, NAS Pensacola, where the ocean let me escape my lonely little life on Merrill Drive. For months, weekend playdates with sand crabs, conch shells, and boogie board waves gave my life meaning until our family of four was under the same roof again.

As I grew older, when my undiagnosed Intrusive Thought Obsessive-Compulsive Disorder (OCD) first waged an angry war against my brain, the only place I could feel any sliver of God was on a splintered dock off the moggy bottoms of Pooler, Georgia. This countrified county outside of Savannah embodied life's good and bad, boasting regal Spanish moss but never camouflaging its pungent papermill smell. My great-aunt owned a lake house there, with a bright green backyard featuring a mucky estuary that housed baby gators, baby sharks, and other grimy creatures that weren't so baby.

My mind was never still, nor were the cranes and fish as they flew and flopped across the brackish waters, but something about water's noise quieted my mind—not for long because OCD is never so gracious. Regardless, the brimming marsh stilled my headspace long enough for me to hear a few words from God. And those few words would have to last for confusing, aching months on end until the dock could welcome me once more.

In fact, on lovely days, when I am quite sure God does not demand my constant perfection, I see water as a secure gateway to his presence. After all, Christ entered this soul-parched earth through a young girl's womb, in an amniotic sack of watery fluid, that helped him grow little hands that would heal lepers, little legs that would walk on raging seas, a little heart that would break for all of humanity, and little lungs that would breathe resurrection life back into his bones. Christ even launched his earthly ministry by letting a social outcast baptize him in the Jordan River. This moment of life and light marks when God's Spirit swept down and confirmed the world's hopeful wonder by declaring yes, this is the Messiah, the One to redeem the least glorious parts of mankind.

Outside unfortunate seasickness and an occasional shark attack on the news, most of us flock to water, or at least its idea. Water promises joy and life. It guarantees movement, growth, and quiet endurance. But on the flipside of landscapes, we do not do as well with the desert—with spaces that seem to hold nothing for miles and miles, where clay and sand conceal scorpions, rattlers, tarantulas, and all other stomach-churning Reptilia. We let the wastelands and barren dirt fill nothing more than our work computers' screensavers. That's it. After logging off, we are finished with Dehydration Station.

So often, as Christians, we perceive the desert just as the children of Israel did. We recall the rapturous glory when God parted our Red Sea and drowned our enemies in the depths, but we let our ability to see miracles live strictly in the past. We like to travel from Miracle A to Miracle B, from the Red Sea to the Land of Milk and Honey, without any Babylonians, pitfalls, or reality filling the gaps of life. We like a tangible faith, one that fuels our senses and makes the Bible give away all its secrets by Genesis 1:2. Wandering in the unknown is an intimidating adventure, especially when we feel we are roaming around a sandy ghost town for days, months, and even years.

Whether we loathe the desert or not, it is, indeed, where all of us eventually find ourselves. Rich or poor, young or old, black or white, male or female, not one member of human society is permitted to skip life's hardships. Regardless of how righteous we live or how promiscuous we may be, we are each subject to the reality of a fallen world.

Realizing the rugged terrain surrounding us, we must accept how limited we are and how dependent we are on something, or Someone, outside the domain of our distress. If we once perceived ourselves omniscient, the desert will surely humble us as we cannot say which way guides us safely home. Furthermore, we often cannot recall how long we have been wandering this wilderness, unsure whether the grace in our souls is depleted.

A culmination of bad decisions, unfortunate circumstances, and waves of unexpected change force us into the middle of nothing, where we feel our life holds no meaning, no value, no purpose. Life is kind of here, kind of there, but no matter which way we turn our heads, the desert offers a tedious, empty view devoid of promise. We find ourselves thirsty, grabbing at any bottle, tipping it up, and praying it gives us life. We find ourselves scared, tiptoeing down each self-blazed trail in fear something might bite us, someone might poison us, and everything else will leave us lifeless. We burn out in the daytime and feel hollow and cold at night. All existence opposes thriving, let alone inviting.

Ironically, it is in the eye of the arid wasteland, in its most futile, cavernous core, where most of God's biblical heroes discovered him. Here, they found his glory not because the land was brimming with sustenance and reliable resources but because these lionhearts were tired, hungry, and in a desperate pursuit of holiness that far surpassed their abilities. Think of Abraham, Jacob, Moses, Joshua, and even John the Baptist—all endured earth's harshest climates and stepped away from their self-made retreats to hear the Lord and discover his plan for their lives.

Abraham was commanded to take his miracle child far away from camp, outside the boundaries of home, and offer him as a sacrifice to the Lord. Though Abraham's obedience spared Isaac, this story solidified the promise of the Lamb to come. After fleeing from his brother Esau, Jacob found himself surrounded by empty land. Yet, it was here that Jacob wrestled with the angel (believed to be the Holy Spirit of God) and was blessed with the vision of angels climbing the ladder to and from heaven. Combined, Moses and his prodigy, Joshua, created forty years of faithful leadership to the Lord while serving in the desert, and in due course, Joshua welcomed the children of Israel to their Promised Land. And John the Baptist, a social pariah, spent his days foraging for locusts and wild honey in the desert, away from a rigid religious society whose soul was parched yet refusing John's hopeful prophecy.

God routed them to the one place where they had to face their limitations, the one place they had to admit God, and only God, could provide a promising roadmap. Though the desert choked their pride, this unbounded land supplied the quiet space that made God's voice, his limitlessness, undeniable and fiercely desirable. Here, only here, is where these great men could comprehend God's infinite providence and his miraculous will unfolding in bounds of mercy, grace, goodness, and beauty.

As a carnal believer who, despite my wild, angry, and sarcastic questions, is assured of God's patience and faithfulness, I remain inclined to inquire: if the desert nearly destroys us, why does God drag us there? Surely, another habitat never mandates fierce survival tactics yet holds these truths. After all, Jeremiah 29:11 promises us a future lacking nothing. Meanwhile, just a few verses later, Jeremiah 29:14 says, "'I will be found by you,' declares the Lord, 'and will bring you back from captivity. I will gather you from all the nations and places where I have banished you,' declares the Lord, 'and will bring you back to the place from which *I carried you into exile*'" (emphasis added).

It seems this was God's choice, God's sole intention, to send his children into the abyss of nothing. After all, God did not call Abraham to sacrifice his son by the beach, where hula skirts and umbrella drinks offered spiritual reprieve. Rather, God forced him far away from home; this empty altar miles from security was the only place God would accept Abraham's heavy sacrifice. Later, in Exodus, though God parted the Red Sea, he refused to teleport his children from the desert to the Promised Land. Regardless of centuries of slavery, he required them to traverse the desert for four decades to discover the blessings he had in store.

Why would a good God promise Jeremiah 29:11 and, only a few verses later, confess that exile was a pre-planned part of the narrative? This decision seems nothing like kindness, love, and mercy—like the plan that should "give [me] a future and a hope" (Jer 29:11). This tinkling brass narrative appears unkind, unloving, anything but hopeful. Why would God willfully subject his beloved to such drudgery? Why allow misery yet demand worship?

Deep down, my soul believes this seemingly harsh command mulls over in our finite minds because most of us are on an exhausted, starving pursuit to believe in a God we can not only love but like too, a God whose kindness is everything we ever dreamed it would be and more. Despite our sins, we desire a fantastical fulfillment only granted by a holy adoration of our Creator.

However, we choose to pursue this journey with great hesitation, keeping a safe arm's distance between us and any trying circumstances that come with chasing head-first after God's righteousness. We are desperate for him, which is detrimental, but why does relentlessly loving God leave us hesitant, tired, and weary? In personal reflection, I have discovered that loving Jesus has always felt so easy to us that we neglect to like him. Such relational emptiness creates a fragile, hollow, and dry perception of the character of God, devaluing his all-knowing and all-loving nature.

Let's be honest: loving Jesus is just what we do. This casual, plain, near-boring ritual is in constant reach for a Christian, particularly in American culture, where few of us face shadows of death like starvation, nakedness, and guerilla warfare. This once-a-week motion is hands-on, heart-off, and yet, we challenge God's love. Or worse, we meander through life with a friction-less faith that offers false fulfillment, and our souls never adopt a love that stays true in all things.

Loving Jesus in this lukewarm light bypasses tragedy for the sake of cheap manufacturing. This feeling that fleets once failures arise often keeps its head above water long enough to piece together an ultimate tagline on any Christian acceptance speech, the go-to tattoo for a slightly rebellious believer. Such a surface-level picture of love creates the phrase we like to use on a first date to check off the other person's Christianity box, cushioning anything between those wispy parameters with spiritual fluff.

But liking Jesus? Choosing to latch onto all the pieces of him? Sitting with him for a chalky cup of matcha and embracing anything he gives to us then asks in return? Such a tall order is rarely described as delightful, steady, rhythmic, and effortless as "Jesus loves me. This I know."

Perhaps love, a command inseparable from heavy, selfless responsibility, feels like the easier path because we have always been called to love God and love others. Adopting this lukewarm notion seems pre-packaged with the trail-blazed, religious turf. We blur just getting by with church attendance, all Christian lingo attached, settling for a disengaged idea of God's love. Meanwhile, we devastate our souls by detaching ourselves from love's God-ordained power. Love, in muted light, loses rhythm, rhyme, and reason in our lives. Thus, loving God has never felt like a mysterious, alluring part of his character we must search out. Instead, this "love" is watered down to the routine we must follow to access heaven, resulting in religion and relationship becoming toxic synonyms only God can differentiate in the hearts of man.

We get the t-shirt, get the bracelet, get the love. Check, check, check. But maybe a box remains unmarked, unsatisfied because our souls are refreshed, replenished, and even healed when we learn to like God too. Then, and only then, can we love him in a way that reveals his love will never fail, carrying us through this life and into eternity with an assurance of the hope he provides.

Sequential flow beckons us to ask why such a drastic gap lies between like and love. Surely, these two bonds are synonymous, right? Such an assumption hinges on our view of location, location, location. When we cement our purpose within the bounds of well-marked turf, playing at home field, we become devoted to the game that offers an advantage, sidestepping hard work. We name nostalgia, pride, and comfort as referees. Our resources are plenty; our ability to survive and thrive on our own appears quite manageable. After all, the water cooler is only a few paces away. So, when someone asks, "Do you really, truly love Jesus?" we say, "Of course. It's the best. Who doesn't?".

We find comfort assuming we have mastered our love for Jesus. Why worry about liking God? Yet, amid this flippant assumption, we quietly, unintentionally lose our spiritual grounding.

Our domain is safe—too invulnerable. If I were a betting woman, I would bet no coach has ever built his home field in a place promising no resources, no life insurance, no jubilation. I am positive no state-champion team has plopped its turf on a mound of sand with cacti for field goal posts and dragon lizards for fans. But what if the dragon lizards are meant to be our supporters, our community? What if the winning field goal doesn't always look as bright yellow, sleek, and celebratory as imagined?

To love God and like God, we must embrace a rougher space that houses the pricklier people, the pricklier problems, and the pricklier prizes that will not always give as much as they take. Maybe it is time to step back and assess our location to see if our like for God is trapped in a self-created, chain-linked fence.

No one talks about liking God—not behind the pulpit, not in a small group, nowhere at VBS—so if you are unsure how to assess your like for God, start by discerning your heart for others. Full disclosure: there are plenty of people I love "for the Bible tells me so." (And only because the Bible tells me so.) I love them with gritted teeth and a supply of grace that I must dig for, the kind of merciful supply I cannot restock on my own.

Yet, loving people in this begrudging, shallow way loses the power of intention, the beauty of caring enough to stick around to ask hard questions and endure more complicated seasons. Loving someone enough to embody love's boldest callings requires action and mandates us to play an active role in another's life. And simple action is where liking someone, including God, begins. Loving someone enough to like them is not an easy journey. It is awkward, sometimes frustrating, and always imperfect, but you must like someone to understand them. It's an unavoidable relational stepping stone.

In my impatient, flawed moods, I associate love with what is mandatory, but I parallel liking someone with my freedom of choice. So, when I choose to like someone, I label them admirable, infatuating. When I like a person, my allegiance is immediately eternal. I show up in their life, embarking on a constant journey to discover who they are. I want to see if they are Team Iced Coffee or Team Hot Coffee. I want to know their favorite candle scent and which tea flavor offers vintage memories. I want to see if they have kids and if their parents are still alive. What triggers them? What hurts them? What elates them? Do they believe in Jesus—and if not, what do they chase to offer infinite satisfaction?

These questions, some seemingly shallow, some undeniably profound, are how we find our friends, the friends who become the heroes we salute.

Most of us cling to our heroes not for the glitzy, famous lives they live but for the way they navigate devastation, the way they refuse to let doubt and destruction dictate their story. Yes, we tend to latch onto the Joan of Arcs and Wonder Women of the world, assuming our infatuation is their beauty and skill with supernova weapons. But if we discern the trustworthy source of our admiration, it stems from the core of who they are, their goodness we cannot see until they face the villains of life.

Thus, the heroes become relatable, teaching us we, too, can embody bravery and courage despite hardships. Sure, our fandom will crave their signature muscle t-shirt. But what makes a hero, a hero, a true friend, a friend, is the spaces they willingly run headlong into while everyone else sprints the other way. The hardships they welcome to ensure others' safety. The soul doesn't require satisfaction from the finite when infinite wisdom is forever available to chase. As a result, we can choose love even when we don't fully understand why God allows villains to tear down cities and souls.

When I like someone, when I have found my hero, a piece of me craves to mirror who they are. Furthermore, when I like someone, I choose to remain with them through the dark seasons, showing up however I can because I not only admire their strength, but I desire to learn from their perseverance.

Such pure imitation births the journey toward fulfilling a genuine like for God—we love him enough to remain when those who promised to stand with us flee, when the skies turn black, volunteering to mirror his Son's sacrifice on the tree. However, it took bleak years of trial and error for me to embrace this truth.

Maybe I lagged in effort because I grew up in a church that made lots of rules as it went, all for the sake of fear-induced control. Though I have loved God for nearly fourteen years, I was petrified to like him with my whole heart until a few years back. As a perfectionist who assumed God functioned as rigidly as I do, I feared messing up. Dodging his (nonexistent) lightning bolts, I never got close enough to have open, honest conversations with him. I holed up in the safe, comfortable shallow end—my home turf—bypassing any beginning stages of a real relationship. I would quickly mutter, "Yep, I love you, Jesus," check that box, and move on my way, continuing to love him, but not like him, all while still living a "good enough" Chrisitan life.

In short, I was not personal with God, and though I claimed to love him, my heart was vacant. I preferred him as a hero stuck in the confined pages of a comic book. I was afraid that if I allowed him to be honest, his kindness might not match his stamina. I was told God was good—but what if he wasn't?

It is quite effortless to love someone you do not live with, yet my self-ish, muted acquaintance with the God who hand-fashioned each fiber of my being continued to wane. Meanwhile, my spiritual tires spun in circles, taking my soul nowhere. Loving him with the checkmark love was more straightforward and less tricky. And less challenging. I was still thirsty for what mattered while never conversing with my personable, gracious Creator. I never let him see me. I rarely shared the daily-grind realities:

I never told God when I was angry, whether my fury was aimed toward him or other people.

I never asked God hard questions because I thought I should not only know but blindly cling to the answers.

I never laughed with God, a stranger to shaking my head in light-hearted dismay when one of my silly mistakes caused an awkward blunder.

I never wept with God over intimidating loss because I was told perfect love should have already cast out my fear. Meanwhile, I was cloaked in self-induced punishment which 1 John 4 warded from believers.

I always kept God far, far away, letting him remain in heaven, not wanting to ask if he would abide with me—because what if he said no? Or worse—what if he said he had already tried to abide with me, but my flaws forced him away?

When you tiptoe around the God you are scared to like, may I let you in on a bit of a secret? You do not love him the way he intended you to. God is too kind to count out your worst efforts at love, but his love, the kind he invites you into, is meant to free you to like him. Such love creates an atmosphere where the Holy Spirit whispers, *you can let go now. You can stop checking the boxes. You're good—even when you're not good. Why? Because I am that good at redeeming your bad.*

For over a decade, I was so afraid of being bad that I never did anything good. I lived in a frozen state, a constant space that made me miserably timid, and I learned to be terrified of messing up. Terrified a perfect

God would demand more. This is why checking the boxes seemed to work for so long. They were black and white. There were fewer challenging obstacles to work through. These religious lists offered tangible confirmation that I was good enough, that God could be proud of me.

As a youth, it looked much like: avoid booze, wild boys, and bucking any and all authority.

Check.

As a church musician, the one all could see behind the stage's piano, it labeled itself: don't forget to tithe.

Check.

As a wife, the mandate resounded as: don't scold your husband because he forgot to fold his laundry . . . again.

Another check.

Boxes checked, I could sign on the dotted line where it read, "Yes, Peyton loves Jesus because the checkmarks tell us so."

And all the while, I knew Jesus resurrected from the grave, but I felt unworthy to leave the tomb.

Years later, I have found my checkmarks were no good. They were a shallow attempt to evade the "bad." But the only way out of this growth stunt is for God to let you stumble into the desert—and by "let you," I mean to force you into a place without checkmarks, schedules, clocks, or any comforts of a hollow spiritual routine. It seems harsh to believe God would volunteer us into this sort of exile, but the desert's core is our holy ground.

We gravitate toward religious routines, and unknowingly, we teach our hearts and spirits to put an abrupt stop to investing too much in God. After all, if we start to care too much, there is now something to lose. The unavoidable deserts now require us to traverse their misery with an underlying sense of eternal joy we are not so sure we can muster. If we get too close, if we begin to find out too many good things, there are now even better things we might miss out on while caught in the wilderness, even better things we might mess up:

God is so good, too good, at staying, so he has a back door somewhere, right?

God is so good, too good, at forgiving, so I need to forgive better to keep his forgiveness, right?

God is so good, too good, at loving me, so I'll probably get in trouble for not loving myself, right?

The good news is that we are wrong. Our self-created stigmas distort our perception of who God is. Sin's smoke and mirrors keep us from throwing away the exterior check-box "love," denying us the freedom to like God through eyes of hope, wonder, and fulfillment. But when we fall in love with liking him, life takes root.

A tender warning, however: you cannot expect growth to always look like my field of daisies by the Hogansville highway. Often, but unfortunately, we solely learn to like God while we are in a place, a season, a desert, we would rather avoid, a place that only houses prickly, pointy plants, a place where water is scarce. But let God drive you to that place, that exile, so you can hear him a little louder, see him a little clearer, and like him a whole lot more. Allow God to root his purpose in your soul in a land where you once believed growth impossible.

What do you say, dear reader? Maybe the time is now for us to love God and like him too. Perhaps it is time to pledge allegiance to a God we are still wary of, and in that process—no matter how wild and scary and challenging—we learn to love him in a gentler, surer way. This way grasps the good kind of love that he designed in the first place—even if Love never promises to stop the hard times but invites us to thrive amid them. And from such a purifying journey, perhaps we will genuinely love others, and deep down, we will come to call our desert a well of hope.

Everyday Application:

1. Whether you are in the desert or have already traversed its heat, what are some heart-changing lessons you have learned in exile?

2. Examine your turf, where you navigate your faith today. Is it comfortable, self-pleasing, routine? If so, what rougher space could you embrace? (A volunteer opportunity, a leadership role in your small group, a relationship on the rocks, etc.?)

3. Which big, bold miracle will you claim today, believing it will appear in your future? And deep down, do you think God is good enough that he will come through?

4. Where are you today on a scale of religious love to liking-God love? What steps could you take to like God in a more authentic, trusting way?

Prayer Closet Thought:

Whichever room in your home, swing on your porch, bench at the park allows you to feel God is closest is what I deem your prayer closet. I encourage you to intentionally find this space and consider a humble thought: who is the one prickly person you've felt called to connect with, but from whom your clashing personalities or differences in hobbies, politics, or religion lead you to steer clear? How can you intentionally reach out to them this week?

2

The Pricklier Side of Things

✦

WHEN MY MIND PAINTS a muted picture of exile, it calls for lackluster, pastel paints that brush wary strokes of vacancy into existence, creating a not-so masterful piece of the last place where I would ever want to attempt survival. Though I'm cold-natured and spend all four seasons cocooned in a sweatshirt and fuzzy socks, the tundra isn't my biggest fear. I'm no stranger to stinging bugs and sticky humidity, so lobbing me into a deep, smoldering jungle wouldn't invoke internal woe. It's the desert that does it for me. My brain plays out a scene with the sun beaming a steaming misery on rough, sandy ground. Tumbleweeds roll past prickly cacti, and scorpions desperately crawl after shade provided by jagged, sun-faded rocks—no sign of life. Water is impossible to reach, whether you trek forward or dig down. None of life's resources are accessible—for miles and miles and miles.

Amid this demised picture, though, I must admit that I'm fascinated by cacti. They not only survive barren, rocky land, but they produce blooms too. Cacti don't rely on surrounding circumstances to sustain life, nor do they settle for merely existing. Instead, they understand their purpose is to give life, and rather than scraping by with a few brown, lifeless patches here and there, they weather the sandstorms surrounding them and still choose to produce beautiful flowers. They don't grow angry at their uncontrollable situation. None of them shoot prickly needles at the heavens because they cannot sprout legs and run from their condition. No, they choose growth. They produce pink, red, white, and yellow petals and bring vitality to an otherwise lifeless landscape.

Out East, you don't stumble into cacti basking in their natural habitat. You either buy them at a store and plant them in your yard or buy one of those mini neon-colored ones and stick it on your windowsill. Regardless of where we Atlantic Coast natives purchase these guys, there's nothing authentic about seeing cacti in the Southeast. However, cacti are cheap and easy to keep alive. As natural survivors of the desert, high maintenance isn't their game. They only require sunlight, which I had plenty of growing up in Georgia.

My dad has the green thumb in our family, but all my mom, my sister (Olivia or "Livz"), and I have to do is look at a succulent the wrong way, and it willingly gives up the ghost in twenty-four hours. Given my dad's military career, he was rarely home, so it had to be cacti if we wanted any greenery in our front yard. Our family planted several cacti around the base of our mailbox, and much to everyone's joy, they survived winter, spring, summer, and fall. Better yet, they endured under the care of the Black Thumb Queens. Unfortunately, this delight wouldn't last forever, not when these cacti would induce one of the most traumatic moments of my and Livz's childhood.

We were outside riding bikes one afternoon, the sun soft and comforting. I was too young to understand life's real pressures. Livz was too young to write her name. There wasn't much to fret on that particular day . . . until Livz fell off her bike and landed in the mailbox's bed of cacti.

If memory serves me correctly, she was riding her pink bike, the princess one with training wheels and glittery streamers on the handlebars. She had turned the slight curve around the mailbox too sharply, losing her balance, and instead of eating the pavement like most kiddos, her little legs ate countless cacti needles.

Livz began wailing, rightfully so. I had no clue what to do at around eight or nine years old, but I did know nothing would get done if I just stood there. I scooped her up and ran her down our driveway, her splotchy little legs dangling. Once I found Mom, she ran Livz a hot bath. I stood by the tub while Mom used tweezers to pluck out each little needle, one at a time.

Livz was a trooper. On the other hand, Mom was a wreck, blaming herself for even letting the cacti live on our property. The next time Dad was home, he excavated the prickly plants. Now, purple and pink spring flowers are planted in the mailbox's little garden bed each March. Nothing with bristles, prickles, pokes, or prods is allowed.

Nothing with bristles, prickles, pokes, or prods is allowed. This is most people's mantra, their hope for themselves and their families. We want to navigate life untainted, unphased, and never traumatized by anything that happens. We crave bliss because it never challenges our souls; it never forces us to fight for who we are and want to be. Sure, each of us wants regal blooms to show off, boasting that we have created a beautiful life worth envy. Most of us truly desire to be good human beings, but how many of us are willing to withstand the necessary hardships, the desert terrain, to produce the miracle of surviving and making it to the other side, both confident and whole?

In 2 Corinthians 6:3–10, Paul warns that afflictions are impossible to avoid:

> "We put no stumbling block in anyone's path, so that our ministry will not be discredited. Rather, as servants of God we commend ourselves in every way: in great endurance; in troubles, hardships, and distresses; in beatings, imprisonments and riots; in hard work, sleepless nights and hunger; in purity, understanding, patience and kindness; in the Holy Spirit and in sincere love; in truthful speech and in the power of God; with weapons of righteousness in the right hand and in the left; through glory and dishonor, bad report and good report; genuine, yet regarded as impostors; known, yet regarded as unknown; dying, and yet we live on; beat, and yet not killed; sorrowful, yet always rejoicing; poor, yet making many rich; having nothing, and yet possessing everything."

If we follow Christ, we aren't escaping the difficult seasons. We will be tired, hungry, and have our faith tested. People will call us liars, pretend not to know us, and seek to bring sorrow into our lives. Yet, we hold to the confidence that Christ is worth it all. He wants us to bloom, sporting lasting petals that withstand the desert. The blooms wearing their unique colors encourage passersby to say, "Those flowers made it. Even in this scorcher, I wonder what makes them so resilient?". God wants this for us because in this growing and blossoming, "we possess everything" (2 Cor 6:10). We have life, the sort of breath in our spirit that can never be snatched away regardless of the landscape. Our beauty is eternal not because of our surroundings but because of the God who rests within us.

One of the fascinating features of the cactus isn't visible from the outside. If you open up a cactus, you will find lots of water. If any plant had a brain, I'd bet on the cactus. It knows its home, the desert, never lets up. The days are scorching, and the nights are freezing. Even worse, the winter season guarantees no rain for months on end. Cacti don't lap all of late fall's water instantly to combat this hazard. Instead, they drink some and absorb most, stocking up to an average of four months' water supply at a time. (Some species of cacti can hold up to two years' supply of water at once.) Cacti have a waxy, inner solid wall that allows them to hold onto the water, shielding them against the sun's blazes that would otherwise force the cacti to use up their reserve.

No one refers to the Holy Spirit as "waxy," but the rubber inner wall of the cactus reminds me of his preservation. The outside eye can't see its strength, but the Holy Spirit protects us within the walls of man's souls. He shields us against the outside world that tries to wear us out and dry us up. His goal has never been to watch us wilt away. Instead, nothing makes him happier than when we bloom. Now, he is a humble Spirit who never forces us to sprout beautiful petals, but he's also a kind Spirit who weathers our most brutal storms, over and over, and has proven himself faithful.

Meanwhile, in the name of an undying passion unachievable by man, Love offers free will. We can deny the life of the cactus, dismissing its desire to thrive amid rugged ground, but the earth's terrain hinges on a fallen world. The desert isn't the only place sin chokes hope. Such austerity will show up regardless of whether or not you are in the desert, whether or not your soul's perspective shifts to chase after purpose in the face of an unadorned life.

I accepted sin's inevitable poison, fully aware it wreaked havoc wherever it pleased, so I was eager to learn the ways of the cactus. But I think I took eagerness a step too far. For a long time, I assumed I was supposed to enjoy the trials I faced. After all, James tells us to "Consider it pure joy, my brothers and sisters, whenever you face trials of many kinds" (Jas 1:2). But the older I get, the more life I live, I believe Paul and James didn't expect us to throw confetti in our affliction, but they knew if we knew there was a purpose to the pain, we would tap into the Holy Spirit's resources. We could find an endurance to weather a season meant to kill us yet allowed us to grow instead.

I have dear friends who are Buddhist, Muslim, agnostic, etc., but one thing we all have in common is inescapable hard times. Believing or not believing in Jesus won't create a life free of bristles, prickles, pokes, and prods. However, I find it so reassuring that my faith never mandates I withstand hard times in a state of perfection. Instead, I'm only called to say, "God, I can't withstand this, but I know you can. Show me why I'm weathering this so when I get to the other side, I can look at others in the same position and say, 'This is the way. Walk in it'" (Isa 30:21).

Bristles, prickles, pokes, and prods are synonymous with growth in the Christian faith. The hard times promise communion with the Spirit and unity amongst other believers if we invite God's purpose to centerstage. They present an opportunity for us to learn, grow, and, even better, survive tough times to show others the map to freedom.

※ ※ ※

Josh and I are a spontaneous duo. We take last-minute road trips in a heartbeat. We will even buy a school bus and begin renovations with full intentions of making it our permanent home, assuming 700 square feet of space is ideal for years to come. We've adopted dogs, bought stock, and moved houses on a whim. It's just who we are, I guess. To add to this reckless list, Josh and I are currently moving from Colorado and purchasing land in Tennessee to start a farm. Driving our stakes into Tennessee's Smoky Mountains ground has always been an understood plan, but the farm is a more recent idea that has grown on both of us.

Frankly, we have witnessed too many people die of cancer, and we are both convinced so much of this sinister disease stems from the chemically-enhanced foods we eat. We want enough space to grow, harvest, and eat our fruits and vegetables, free of pesticides and poisons. We want land capable of sustaining cows, goats, and chickens to provide us with a fresh, antibiotic-free source of dairy and meat. Best of all? In addition to clean eating, we crave clean air and an open, noiseless space free of car honks and cell phone towers.

Now, there's a slight but significant difference between loud and noisy. Loud tends to call for attention but invokes a purpose. Teachers are loud when calming down a class so students can continue to learn, nurses are loud when reaching the doctor to ensure a patient receives emergency treatment, and God is loud when he wants our attention. On the other hand, noisiness tends to call for attention, but it invokes no purpose. It wants attention for the sake of attention. It's a fleeting climax that plummets as soon as we don't get enough time in the spotlight. Josh and I can handle the loud "cock-a-doodle-doo" of a rooster signaling it's time for us to start the day, but we've grown tired of the car honks and revving engines of daily road rage from folks who zip in and out of traffic so everyone knows they own a sports car.

One of the loud sounds I am most excited to hear on the farm is the bleating of sheep. I knew we would have cows, goats, and chickens, but I never anticipated that Josh would want to add sheep to the cattle mix. Sheep aren't easy creatures to rear. They are fluffy, quiet, and precious babies, but their needs are expensive, time-consuming, and riskier than chickens, goats, and other farm animals.

Sheep are like toddlers who never leave their Terrible Twos behind. That's not to say sheep are ornery and throw constant tantrums, but sheep require round-the-clock care. They must be watched at all times, or else pure chaos—gut-wrenching and expensive chaos—can ensue at any given time.

Sheep are prone to wander off and lack the instinct for how to return home. They also require constant medication as they are highly predisposed to parasites from grass and water. In (a gross) addition, bots fly maggots will invade a sheep's nose and cause them to accidentally kill themselves. They fatally beat their heads against rocks and ground, begging to be free of the insect invasion. This is why David says in Psalm 23:5: ". . . You anoint my head with oil . . ." The only thing that keeps maggots from entering the sheep's nose is a special oil shepherds pour over their heads which runs down their face and into their nose, creating a thick shield from bots fly maggots.

Though purchasing sheep was initially Josh's idea, he thought I would enjoy caring for them. "You could be the shepherdess," he said. "Would you be up for it? Sheep require constant attention." Not sure how I would continue working my day job, milking a cow, collecting eggs, keeping a farmhouse clean, and constantly watching after sheep, I responded, "I would love that!" Why would I love to add one extra task to my daily to-do list? Because this would be my one chance to better understand Jesus as my Shepherd. Sure, I've heard and believe Jesus is constantly with me, guiding me, chasing me down when I'm dumb and stubbornly stomping away from the fold. I know this truth in my head, but to see that and feel it in such a hands-on way would be revolutionary for my faith. I'll name the sheep, discover their personalities, notice their strengths and weaknesses, and in this knowing, I'll love the relentless, repetitive act of saving them from their same silly troubles. And I believe that's how our Shepherd works.

Sure, his omniscience doesn't require him to learn anything about us. His knowledge is all-knowing. But he knows us by name, sees us for our strengths even in the face of our weaknesses, and adores us in the way that giving his life for ours was his heart's greatest desire. As I love on my and Josh's sheep, I imagine that as I name them and distinguish their personalities, I'll have a richer understanding of "The Lord is my Shepherd; I lack nothing" (Ps 23:1).

Reading comprehension begs the question: what do cacti and sheep have in common? One is prickly; one is plush. One lives in the desert, and the other thrives among lush, green land. Well, it's not any of the characteristics that cause them to parallel one other. Instead, it's their resources that tie them together. The cactus has a waxy inner wall that keeps it hydrated, even in the toughest, driest, most barren seasons. The sheep have a shepherd who keeps out coyotes and creates a tight protection barrier around the flock.

Cacti and sheep aren't much on their own. One's a low-maintenance plant meant for black thumb queens, and the other is an ignorant ball of stinky cotton. But, with behind-the-scenes resources, one produces bright, unimaginable flowers amid a desert, and the other survives the threat of wild woods to offer wool as a means of clothing and comfort to all. The cacti can't dodge the desert. The sheep can't pretend coyotes and wolves don't stalk the local woods. Life will still happen for both of them. Hard times won't cut either a break, but because the cacti trust their internal walls and the sheep trust their shepherd, who they are serves a lasting purpose.

The desert will threaten to quench our love for others, especially in hard times. The coyotes and wolves will threaten to tear apart our reputation, relationships, and reason for keeping the faith. But the Great Shepherd will guide us with his rod and staff (Ps 23:4). He will ensure that our cup runs over (Ps 23:5). We will be protected, refreshed, and rehydrated. Come what may, we "will dwell in the house of the LORD forever" (Ps 23:6).

There's a flipside to the pricklier things of life when we give God the reins (or the staff). Miracles happen when we allow a purpose far more selfless than our wants to take root in the most unexpected places. This doesn't mean the path is easy; after all, we can't duck from the desert and those dang coyotes, but faith always guarantees that God holds our place in the fold. Here, we are not only safe but known by name. We are known for our strengths despite our weaknesses. We are loved not because of how we see ourselves or our situations but because the Shepherd finds worth solely in us belonging to him.

Everyday Application:

1. Are you a plant person? If so, what draws you to this botanical hobby? Do you find joy in planting seeds, anticipating growth, and showcasing the beautiful aftermath when buds and blooms burst through? If not, what draws you away from plants? Do you have a black thumb like me? Do you not have the time? Knowledge? Patience?

2. Once you have answered the first question, parallel the attributes to your spiritual walk. (This does not mean that anti-plant people choose to stagnate spiritual growth.) Gardening gurus, do you find joy in planting seeds of faith in others? Do you actively engage hope in your Christian walk as you wait for God to show you his purpose? For the Black Thumb Queens, are you actively practicing patience as you try to understand better the application God seeks from you? Where can you go to glean more knowledge surrounding God's goodness and loyalty?

3. God calls us his sheep, so there is an undeniable attribute to all of us that leans toward the stupid side of things. In what seasons of life have you wandered off, whether for a few minutes of frustration or years of bitterness, and God brought you back home?

4. Does your worth stem from God's desire for you? If not, where are you pursuing worth? How might these other places leave you dry, damaged, distant from the fold?

Prayer Closet Thought:

Botanical babe or not, I encourage you to buy a plant. If you're wary of this feat, start with my favorite neon-pink cacti, the baby kind. Or, if you have plants decorating your home now, find one that requires extra care, one that might challenge your plant knowledge. Note its color, shape, and size. What does it need of you? What abilities does it have so long as you provide proper sunlight and water? Then imagine those possibilities and opportunities you have, even as a sheep, so long as you allow the Shepherd to anoint your head with oil.

3

Wall of Wounds

※

ARE YOU AN ATHLETIC prodigy, born and bred with a brain that knows its way around stamina and agility? Or are you like me, a person who makes posters, buys the ball cap, and cheers on my favorite baseball and hockey teams? Regardless, everyone understands that it's common for a coach to sacrifice his likability so the team will bond off a unified hatred for their ruthless leader. This concept is the precise strategy Coach Herb Brooks infused into his 1980 Winter Olympics U.S. hockey team, who stole an unimaginable victory from Russia, ending the then-USSR's back-to-back-to-back gold medal streak. This U.S. hockey team was one of the youngest of its kind, a rare bunch compiled of boys who were still actively playing against each other in college hockey with fresh vendettas to fulfill on the Olympic practice rink.

Men from the University of Minnesota and Boston University—big-time rivals who were in no mood to wear the same jersey and call each other "teammate"—created a chunk of this twenty-four-man lineup for the stars and stripes, holding little hopes for any success against the real opponents. University of Minnesota's leading hockey player at the time, Rob McClanahan, emphasized this unavoidable college tension while talking with John Shipley of *The St. Paul Pioneer Press*: "It was just a rivalry that existed. Both teams just wanted to beat the crap out of each other."[1]

Few people expected much from this not-so united team. All the U.S. wanted was a non-embarrassing performance from the boys, and anything

1. Shipley, "Miracle on Ice Coverage," para. 7

better would be better than anticipated. Yet, Brooks' torturous practices and abrasive speeches subconsciously taught the hockey players to drop their former grudges against one another and feed all anger toward him. Eventually, as they grew to respect one another, they came to love their "soulless" coach. Talent mixed with a love of game and team brought about a historic victory over the USSR. Their win clenched not only the title but the fascinating truth that internal hardships and tension can breed a rare sort of unity. Since this 1980-win, history has coined these young Olympians the Miracle on Ice team.

Like Brooks' team, we tend to bond with each other over the people and things we loathe. This is how most of our relationships work in life, if you think about it. Recall your middle school days. Note how many of your friends were friends because you both hated the popular girl who came from loads of money and had loads of attitude to match. Fast forward to your college days. How many of your friend groups bonded over the misery of staying up late together to study for the math professor's terrifying exams week after week? Then, you have the office, a place where you buddy up with whoever best understands your complaints as small as the coffee pod options to as grandiose as your boss' snarky need for control. It is easier to feed off each other's negativity because negative energy never calls anyone to do better, be better, and break the life-sucking cycle. All negative energy requires to thrive is more negative energy.

The deeper I dig into this concept of bonding over mutual hate for another person or thing, the more I believe these bonds run less on hatred and more on people uniting with those who have similar wounds—often, *unhealed* wounds.

In so many ways, this is how I see the children of Israel stumbling through the desert. Though Aaron was the official religious leader of God's people, he was too cold-footed to harvest Herb Brooks' results. Aaron liked being liked, and when your sole pursuit is pleasing wounded people rather than helping them heal, you learn the hard way that no one changes for the better. Likeability for the sole sake of likeability never levies anything deeper than watered-down allegiance. In Aaron's case, people-pleasing created a more formidable body of people. He threw flimsy bandages on their gaping wounds, never addressing the hard things, and yet, he wondered why they never relinquished their complaints.

Meanwhile, Moses cast himself in the role of Leader Everyone Hates. He was the only one willing to disregard his popularity and pour antiseptic on Israel's wounds. He knew healing was a painful process, but it was worth it, even if it meant not being the fan-favorite.

While the children of Israel's constant grumbling pestered Moses, he extended truth and grace because he knew these were unhealed, un-whole, scarred people. Though whiny, their bonds forged with blood that ran deep into their bones, into who they had become. In the name of authentic leadership, Moses was always willing to take the brunt of their humanity, always ready to dish out the rules no one wanted to follow, so long as these hurt people remembered the goodness of God. Moses sacrificed his status, even his likability, so Israel would not only remember but choose to accept Jehovah Rapha, the God Who Heals.

Most of Brooks' boys were quietly struggling with the wounds of personal tragedies in school and at home. Most, if not all, Israelites were struggling with injuries of whippings and beatings and wounds of feeling as if a good God wouldn't have left them to suffer for so long. And most of us in modern-day society struggle with countless wounds of our own:

Social media propels our feelings of inadequacy and jealousy. Fear hangs in thick clouds above a world that might forever live in pandemic-induced panic. Fragile trust becomes a guarded safety net after being neglected and abandoned too often. Then church drama, childhood trauma, and every mental and physical health problem in between snatch a list of undeserving victims.

In summary, we are sometimes the reason for each other's wounds, we are often the reason we can't let our wounds heal, and we are always the ones who choose whether or not to build walls around our wounded souls with the brick and mortar of faults and fears. This is where I believe unhealed wounds are left wide open. We can't let go of our weaknesses and fear an unforeseeable future.

Hindsight conveniently urges us to yell at Israel: "You just saw God part the Red Sea—what's your problem?". However, we often view their fear from the wrong angle. Yes, the desert provided natural fear; the Israelites wondered where food, water, and the Promised Land lived, understandably. But I believe the Israelites were most afraid of old spiritual wounds they had never extended the grace to heal.

If they had adequately wrestled with God like Jacob did when he said, "I will not go unless you bless me" (Gen 32:26), they would have witnessed God's goodness and sovereignty reign true. They would have found peace with the past and a strange sweetness among their scars. Jacob's permanent limp after wrestling left him with more assurance of God's enduring presence. Meanwhile, the Israelites' suffering in the wilderness held an eternal weight to carry them home. God's presence doesn't negate hardships; it ensures each ounce of our suffering serves a refining purpose filled with hope.

They had access to the God who told the Red Sea to make way for his children, the God who faithfully sent a light—the Light—to guide them day and night. Yet, they distorted their perspective of God's sovereignty by peering at his plan through the cracks and crannies of their walls of un-healed wounds. Their faults and fears left them walking in sluggish circles, going nowhere.

Faults are gritty to face because they are self-inflicted. When we mess up, we have to pay the price. Yet, too often, even after paying the earthly price, we refuse to drop the spiritual weight and recognize that we are free of shame. If you steal money from a store, you go to jail. That's how an imperfect world works. But the moment your soul is convicted, and you repent of your fault, God forgets it even happened.

However, just like a physical jail cell, we keep ourselves locked in a mental cage, assuming God forces us to spend a minimum of fifteen years behind our shameful bars. We think freedom is only meant for the righteous ones and until we've paid our dues, there's no hope for us. This is where I struggle most. While I carry the fear that stems from the broken promises and failed relationships onset by others, what I don't handle as well is when things go wrong, and I'm the facilitator of destruction.

Perhaps it's because I am a perfected perfectionist. Or maybe OCD is to blame with raging, incessant thoughts always whispering, *you gotta do better than that, girl*. Or, the devil knows my weak spot and enjoys punching me where it hurts most. I am sure it's a combination of all three, but I can only fight my wounds that thrive on obsessing over flaws by holding them up to the light of God's Word. I have found no outside space to access such peace and rest.

Yes, this seems cliché, but when I say "God's Word," I am not referring to Jeremiah 29:11. Often, when you feel bad, the "feel good" verses in the Bible are like salt in the wounds. It seems complicated to relate with biblical authors because they watched God shut the mouths of lions. They were the eye-witnesses of water becoming wine, sight restored to the blind, and death transformed into life. Meanwhile, you grapple for a nudge of hope about a job interview or a second date. Instead of the happy verses, let's discuss the much heavier, less light verses Jeremiah wrote in Lamentations—a book of literal lamenting. This is the Jeremiah commonly coined as the "weeping prophet." This is Scripture's open dialogue between God and a disheveled, fearful prophet.

In Lamentations 3, Jeremiah is in a place of doubt, silence, hurt, confusion, and utter frustration. God charged him to point the Tribe of Judah toward his refining law, but if you know anything about the Tribe of Judah, it's no shock to discover they never received an A in conduct on their report card. Here, Jeremiah's soul is heavy after wrestling with the sick spirits of Judah. He feels beaten, all energy depleted. In verses 10–15, Jeremiah mourns the hope he believes is lost. Here, not only has he not heard from God in quite some time, but he feels as if God has poured out all wrath meant for Judah on him:

> "Like a bear lying in wait,
> Like a lion in hiding,
> He dragged me from the path and mangled me
> And left me without help
> He drew his bow
> And made me the target for his arrows.
> He pierced my heart
> With arrows from his quiver.
> I became the laughing stock of all my people;
> They mock me in song all day long.
> He has filled me with bitter herbs
> And given me gall to drink."

Jeremiah truly believes God has mangled him and left him for dead—all hope, all light, all life, gone forever. But, a big, beautiful, bursting ball of light and life can be found in that same chapter only a few verses later:

> "Yet this I call to mind
> And therefore I have hope:
> Because of the LORD's great love we are not consumed,
> For his compassions never fail.
> They are new every morning;
> Great is your faithfulness.
> I say to myself, 'The LORD is my portion;'
> Therefore I wait on him . . .
> For no one is cast off
> By the Lord forever.
> Though he brings grief he will show compassion
> So great is his unfailing love.
> For he does not willingly bring affliction

Or grief to anyone" (v 21–24, 31–33).

Just as Jeremiah discovered, we must realize hurt, pain, and grief are not of God. However, instead of letting us walk through life free of these things, God chooses to offer compassion instead. God chooses to suffer with us. He craves our allegiance even if we stumble through our desert with ratty baggage. He desires to walk with us in these times, too, freeing us of our wounds and tearing down any walls we have built in the name of our faults and fears.

God created a unity with us forged from a mutual understanding of hurt and pain. He is a hands-on God whose limitless love faced the worst of anything we would ever go through. When we see Jesus as more than a loud-mouth coach with a book complete in rules and see him as a God who chose the weight of our shame, we become our Miracle in the Desert sort of team. God and us versus anything life's worst might hurl our way.

A prophetess I am not, but I urge you in this holy pursuit. Make room for healing, realizing that your mistakes and your fears don't dictate whether or not you deserve ever to be whole again. God decided you were worth grace millennia ago when he sent his Son to take history's worst wounds so you and I would never have to. He made sure that when the veil of the temple was torn, we had the same power through the Holy Spirit to tear down our walls of wounds, the veils hiding our insecurities.

Reflecting on the crucifixion and resurrection, I cannot escape how Jesus chose to keep his scars. As the perfectly resurrected Messiah, his exit from the tomb and earth could have been flawless. He could have chosen to look like Hercules with a glittering body. Instead, Christ chose to remain in his wounds for all eternity. He decided to remember his wounds to get down in the dirt with us as we dismantle shame and dig for hope on the other side of faults and fears.

Though my walls hold no theological degrees, a peaceful fervor hums in my spirit and leads me to believe when we first embrace our Savior on the other side of this world, he will show us his wounds. We will see his scarred hands and feel them. We will touch the hole in his side. No doubt, we won't require the same reassurance as Thomas, but we will all need the soft, gracious reminder that if Jesus walked with us on earth and brought his scars to heaven, we are worth glory road's citizenship.

I ponder Jeremiah's lament in Lamentations 3. When I daydream of my King, who chose never to be free of his scars, I realize the unhealed pieces of me aren't meant to close me in, to keep me in a tight wall where

I never face life, never trust love again. While these concepts are easy to accept as nothing more than feel-good, fleeting thoughts, I can chip away at my wall of wounds, bitterness, and hate by writing a letter to my faults and fears—all of my mistakes. My blunders live in the past. Yet, I address them in the present since the weight of their existence often remains so noisy and vivid in my shamed heart. After all, Jeremiah dedicated an entire book to declaring God's beauty from ash.

Full of total vulnerability, while writing this chapter, I felt much like Jeremiah. I hadn't heard from God in days, and I was afraid the static was my fault, that my failures were to blame. Yet, choosing to believe in Christ's character, I could press through the enemy's lies. I found solace in writing a letter to my mistakes, affirming that they hold no power in light of God's love. That letter, the one that brought this chapter to life, reads:

Dear Past Mistakes,

Even in the present, you are fresh and new—but not in a glamorous way. Your holes remain deep, your wounds wide, and I am left waiting and wondering when healing will begin. I am eager to face the sting of disinfecting, disentangling my flaws. Letting my biggest mistakes bubble and brew until they're gone. For my numb soul, pain is worth the cleanse.

A portion of my being feels rude for assuming healing is something that will happen. After all, it's something I don't deserve. But every other time I falter, I find God is still here. His eyes still kind and his hands still patching up the worst of me.

I'll be honest, Past Mistakes, I already feel I've messed up too big, in the sort of ways that leave me wondering if my prayers are reaching heaven. It's not that I've taken on the title of murderer, robber, or cheater, but the darkest parts of my heart have a way of inviting me into subtle rebellion. Unfortunately, for the sake of my schedule and agenda, I often buy into a lifeless cause, the wrong sign, the wrong words, and only allow hindsight to stir conviction too late. Serving self, denying anything and everyone else, is a stumbling block I know too well.

I don't feel God at the moment. I'm not sure I have heard his voice in almost a week. What's worse is I'm not sure when I will hear from him again. Or what if I hear from him again and don't know it's him? My thoughts can't be trusted with an overly imaginative, hyper-negative mental condition like

OCD. Often, it takes days, weeks, even months, and years to separate which thoughts are mine and which are a lie.

But I don't have months and years, even days and weeks, to discover whether or not grace is mine for the taking. I want it, need it, and crave it in the here and now. And as I think about you, Past Mistakes, I can't neglect the darkness you bring. Yet, if I consider darkness, I must weigh the other side of your existence.

It's a relentless struggle to accept truths you don't deserve, but I must remember light and life are God's, and these gifts are present for each of us, regardless of mistakes, no matter how deep into darkness our souls have wandered.

Allowing hope to lead, Past Mistakes, I recall what brought Jesus to earth. Not that Jesus didn't know our sorrow—his sovereignty knows no limits. But something about the empty state our mistakes leave us in led him to walk among us. He didn't only want to know our need, but he wanted to know our desperation for grace. Perhaps that made it easier for him to face the prophecy of his sacrifice, or maybe empathy is the selfless way he chooses to connect with us.

Past Mistakes, your death-grip circulates through my body, threatens my breath. You have crippled me in silent ways, catching me off guard in the quietest places I can't escape. Despite your upper hand, though, I must admit: God won. He triumphed over you.

Oddly enough, you met your demise in the book of Lamentations, the book where Jeremiah's soul feels tortured and tarnished without any hope of reaching the other side. It seems strange to find victory in a book of lamenting. Yet, Lamentations 3 reveals Jeremiah's decision to bank on the Lord's goodness, on God's light and life, regardless of the darkness surrounding him. Jeremiah recognized his own mistakes and knew how often he had pursued the wrong direction. Even still, something about the hope of God reminded him that darkness is defeated forevermore thanks to the wondrous resurrection of the Messiah, a resurrection Jesus chose to embody with his scars fully intact, visible for eternity.

We have room to feel conviction and wrestle with our mistakes, but we give guilt to God after the fight. From there, we relinquish self-torture. We were never called to wriggle and writhe in the misery of faults already forgiven by the Creator.

Past Mistakes, I say all that to say this: you are a wall coming down in the name of Jesus. Your bricks are too heavy, but no burden is too heavy, no barrier too high, for my God to take down.

Would your letter resemble mine? Do faults make up most of your wound wall? Or is fear your self-destructive game? Perhaps you don't personify your mistakes and then write letters to them, but I hold sad confidence you have one big mistake, or tons of tiny ones, that feel so real you remain convinced they are animate. Your faults take up too much space, stack far too high, to not live your life for you. Fear invades your breath, each one a long, heavy sigh. They weigh down your shoulders; your body bent in defeat. They operate from the inside until the mind, body, and spirit freeze with bleak fear.

It's a strange feeling as a believer to take up hollow space behind life-less walls but know that God is in the emptiness you occupy despite feelings. He sits beside you, begging you to step into a truth you know too well to ignore: "I will never leave you nor forsake you" (Deut 31:6).

Whether you are a church native or still contemplate Christianity, I have a secret: your faults and fears can't and won't dictate God's omnipotent character. Don't give your flaws that much credit. Never allow the brick-and-mortar fears to stack intimidation so high. Remember, God's thoughts birth galaxies. His smile calms seas. His soul stoops in adoration for the creatures he made by hand. That's me. That's you. And just as he knows the parameters of the Milky Way and the exact spot the ocean stops, he knows our limits too.

Unfortunately, our limits look messier, much more wounded than shooting stars and broken shells. When we shoot for the stars, our landing isn't glorious as bright-light wonder. No one stops and makes a splendid wish when they see us aim high and fall. They might laugh, might love that our failure boosts their shallow ego, but they won't elbow their friends and whisper, "Did you see that?! Wasn't it beautiful?". When life's storms beat us up and spit us on dry ground, no beauty calls for kids to pitter-patter bare-foot down the sand and collect tiny treasures. Nothing glorious remains but mucky seaweed tangling our best efforts.

Recall Moses, the Leader Everyone Hates. But, this time, it's Jesus. Jesus was the leader who never prioritized being liked over showing others love. For thirty-three years, he gave up his home in heaven to walk among the faults of mankind. Christ chose to become acquainted with our pressures, stressors, and triggers. He decided to face our wall of wounds with grace and mercy. Our wall of wounds is why he came. Christ's crucifixion didn't just rip the temple veil, but it tore down shame, and in his resurrection, he kept the scars as a reminder that healing is forged in a love we would never know without our wounds.

Beauty from ash, dear reader. Wide-eyed wonder from wounds. Salvation from scars.

Everyday Application:

1. Take stock in your friendships. Notice who you choose to engage in conversation, time, and energy. Do you stay close to them to justify your frustration or feed your pain and anger? If so, perhaps it's time to allow this friendship to take a more willing, optimistic approach.

2. When you are in a challenging space, do you get agitated with the "feel good" verses? I know I often do. I encourage you to take these verses in a greater context. Are you reading the whole chapter? Do you know what the author survived to share the "feel good" hope?

3. How can you relate to Jacob when he wrestled with the angel (Gen 32:22–32)? Just as Jacob refused to give up the fight until God blessed him, are you relentless in your pursuit of God's presence?

4. How will you actively pursue showing others love over being liked? Especially in today's social media-influenced culture?

Prayer Closet Thought:

Perhaps it's time for you to write a letter to your past mistakes. Yes, writing a letter to a non-tangible might feel strange, but once you finish, you will discover you've often been hearing from God, day in and day out. But, unfortunately, you have yet to get past your mistakes to hear anyone, Anyone, else.

4

Hay and Healing

※

ARE THERE PLACES YOU have visited that your brain never wants to re-map? The sort of spaces that even Siri volunteers to forget because they embody such gray, bleak memories? The spots engulfed with loss? I have quite a few, but three stick out as the sorest of sore thumbs:

Berry College: This beautiful, rural campus in Rome, Georgia, hosts hundreds of acres filled with wild deer and even castles. Yet, with undiagnosed OCD, my first semester of college felt less like a castle and more like a dungeon. Trapped in my thoughts and fears, I was afraid to get out and spend time with my roommate, classmates, and others. I had the chance to join a swing-dancing club, a Bible study, and other organizations. Yet, my mind convinced me I was safer if I stayed away from anything outside the comforts of my car. I was less likely to mess something up if I separated myself from people altogether.

After five months of being away from family but ever-present in my darkest headspace, I packed up my bags and went home. I returned the matching comforter from my roommate. I threw away all Vikings t-shirts, magazines, and memorabilia. I even deleted 90 percent of my new Facebook friends from there, ashamed they could piece together why I left. Now, Berry College is nothing but a host of sad, defeating memories, the sort of remembrances that still whisper, *you failed.*

Certain relatives' homes: This is a tough one. I don't speak to several members of my family. Unfortunately, the way they treated my father, mother, and little sister, who was always too young and naive to be manipulated by family drama, has left a bitter taste in my mouth. Time and time again, they continued to remind me that blood isn't always thicker than water, but instead, love runs deeper than them all. And without love, the God-ordained concept of family is entirely lost.

Over the years, I've worked through the bitterness, recognizing that true freedom comes from forgiving and moving on. Their unwillingness to change their temperamental, cruel ways has left me no choice but to keep a social distance from them, protecting mine and my family's spiritual, mental, and emotional health.

The Waffle House off Commerce Road: This Waffle House, only five minutes from my childhood home, is where I would meet up with two of my best friends from high school who remained dear friends in college. One night each week, we would meet there around midnight and hang out until three in the morning. It was a time for laughs, unhealthy food, and the chance to catch up on the week's latest drama.

Unfortunately, one of those dear friends went through a hard, hard season shortly after college, and to be frank, I didn't navigate that season as a good friend should. I asked about her instead of showing up at her door to absorb her pain as my own. I settled for a near-gossip-like "How is she?" over "Hey, I'll be at your door in five minutes with coffee." Ties severed— ties disappeared altogether. Now, that rundown, forever dirty Waffle House reminds me of when I didn't show up for someone who needed me most, a time when I chose selfishness over empathy. And I miss my red-headed best friend, who never forgot how much I loved anything lemon-flavored, who showed me how to heat an eyelash curler so the curl would last all day. I'll forever regret that I didn't remember her pain in the present. I didn't show up but chose to show out instead.

I hate to ask, but could you call out, maybe even write out, your own spaces like these? Perhaps a spot that reminds you of a failed job, friendship, or marriage? Or perhaps you can bring to mind a location that tore apart your ability to trust anyone, anything—even the church?

Once you have your list, and you've defined why these places remain so heavy, the next step, the step where we find healing, is to realize that Jesus already took care of this third and final step. Finding peace with the past, discovering rest in today's crazy world, and accessing freedom from worrying about the future all rely on the healing hands of God. The third step is as simple as recalling who God is, who he has shown himself to be repeatedly.

God began the journey of putting mankind's hurt to rest in a place that no one would ever want to step into, a setting where no one would ever want to discover their purpose. He turned the world upside down and set law and love in order by sending the Messiah to us in a dingy, stinky manger.

Thanks to modern-day graphic design, we can avoid the places we hold most miserable. We can project the grossest of sites in a beautiful light too. If we have to remember those places, we can photoshop them, creating them into something less embarrassing, less cringeworthy. We can sidestep any bad, scary, defeating memories that make a space less inviting. Take the Nativity, for example:

We can imagine a manger stuffed with plush, yellow hay, forgetting that animal slobber, dirt, and more brittle layers of straw were Christ's place to rest his head. We can picture Joseph standing over the manger with broad, proud shoulders, not knelt next to his wife after days of being on his feet, covered with blisters and carrying the question of how to rear a promise, the Promise, that no one else believed. Then we can portray Mary as the woman with flawless wavy hair and a gentle, near-angelic glow, not as a scared, naive young girl covered in sweat and blood from the raw beginnings of motherhood.

When we picture pivotal places with all the beauty but without the ash—or forcefully forget those settings altogether—we no longer connect the gaps they fill, the hearts they heal, the harvest they gather from heavy places. Why are we so willing to run headlong against things meant to make us whole? Because growth must anticipate death and still choose to grow despite the loss.

If we go back to the manger, the Nativity as a whole, there is a beautiful, all-around sacrifice that made way for the Gift of all gifts:

Mary and Joseph both died to their reputations.

The shepherds knew what it meant to lose a sheep to a wolf.

The wisemen gave up months with their loved ones, losing memories never made, all in pursuit of a star.

The animals—all the cows, donkeys, chickens, and any critter in between—gave up their beds, feeding troughs, and home.

The baby gave up heaven, his rightful place by the Father. He chose to lose everything because mankind's soul was on the line. And for Christ Jesus, despite knowing the brutal death he would endure, he knew loss was worth growth. The resurrection power, on the other side, was worth his pain.

Jesus wanted to free us from idolizing a reputation, keeping up an image for imperfect people who would never be satisfied with our performance.

Jesus wanted us free from the wolves, the enemy, nipping at our heels, begging us to believe lies.

Jesus wanted us free from following a lifeless routine from the rise and fall of the sun so we could observe the Maker of the galaxies.

Jesus wanted us to know that we would forever have a home, forever be full and satisfied, in his presence.

His loss was mankind's gain. His death mankind's life. And for him, he chose our growth at the expense of his loss.

What an honor for us to follow suit. Thankfully, we don't have to endure the agony of crucifixion. Still, we have the privilege of walking through loss with the hopeful perspective that something brighter, something worth it all, is on the other side. Even more fundamental, God allows us to stumble through these seasons of growth when we are running on fumes, when we are tired, hungry, and halfway scared to pray big prayers.

It's hard to imagine how growth can be born from such isolating, desolating places, and yet, it's when our resources are lost, when we've faced death in every way, that growth takes root. Healing sprouts when we see God blooming beautiful things from dry ground. And that, my dear friend, is the reason we can stand on a pile of ash, in a pit of sand, in a wasteland, in the places of our worst mistakes and memories, and boldly proclaim, "He is a God I'll die to live for."

While I'll never have the honor of birthing baby Jesus, I understand what it means to die to reputation. As the endearing wife who traveled the world with her husband, the writer who flourished in a career blogging and speaking, I always checked the boxes, aced the tests, and did the right thing. My reputation and social media image were impenetrable, and I'm sure all on the outside believed I was happy. But once my OCD grew too strong, once I ended up in a therapist's office spilling my ugliest, scariest thoughts, I knew it was time to die to my reputation. It had grown into an idol that blocked any ability to grow.

Dying to my reputation wasn't natural. It didn't feel comfortable. I was afraid that admitting this diagnosis would open my soul to a world known too well for its judgments and gossip. I was worried people wouldn't believe me. I was anxious that they might assume I had jumped on the "mental health train" to chug through life with an excuse. But the total opposite happened. Instead, I found a community that came behind me and cheered me on, a group of people who would send private messages and texts sharing their similar experiences with mental health struggles. We found God's hope through each other's ruins. Though OCD was found guilty as the imposturous murder weapon that stole my reputation, I found life on the other side of pleading guilty to my most significant flaw.

❊ ❊ ❊

An avid animal person, from dogs to giraffes to sharks (just the Hammerhead kind), one of my favorite stories of near-impossible victories stars Maggie, my parents' Dachshund and Pug-mixed pup. Formally known as Magnolia Mae, Maggie is the most rachet punk. Weighing in at a mean twelve pounds, this bug-eyed furball bullies my parents' ninety-pound German Shepherd. She steals his treats and buries them. She snatches his toys and claims them as her own. Allow me to reiterate: she's a terror, a tornado of snarls and slobber, but she's a fighter. And I've always had a thing for fighters.

The Dachshund breed is known for struggling with back pain. After all, their accordion torsos create plenty of opportunities for injury, and Maggie inherited that slinky trait from the Dachshund side of her family. On Christmas Day 2018, she decided to lunge off my parents' back deck, possibly in pursuit of a neighborhood cat, but the landing didn't go as planned. About two days later, Auburn University's vet clinic showed us an x-ray of her spinal cord, revealing bits and pieces of shattered vertebra scattered throughout her back. Surgery was crucial, a painstaking six-hour procedure that wouldn't guarantee her life. Even though my Maggie survived surgery, the next two weeks were rockier. While it wasn't abnormal for dogs to pull through this type of surgery, it wasn't uncommon for them to pass away over the next several weeks, their bodies unable to withstand the initial trauma.

Josh and I were married, and I was no longer living with my parents, but even still, we all took turns on Maggie patrol, ensuring she didn't roll over or overexert herself. We held her, cried over her, prayed over her in ways I didn't know humans could pray for dogs. Thanks to the God of miracles, Maggie pulled through those two weeks. Yet, her vet team consistently pressed that she would never walk again; her two back legs would never move.

But no one in my family would accept that. My dad began taking her to our local vet for water therapy, where they would place her in a bathtub of warm water with a conveyor belt-type aquatic treadmill. Dad and the vet techs would pick up her floppy back legs, hand-forcing little bicycle kicks. Week after week, everyone would cheer on her water therapy journey, begging for any signs of movement yet anticipating the worst. Finally, Maggie's back two legs picked up the tiniest of motions, and over time, she eventually regained the strength to stand on them. Years later, Maggie is walking and running on those two back legs. Granted, it's a catawampus kind of walk and run, and when she tuckers out, she scoots around on her front two legs, flip-flopping across the floor like a seal. But this tenacious miracle, the willpower to believe this miracle would happen, pulled our fur family through.

Our belief in miracles only showed up due to trauma, of our family being in a place we would rather not revisit. We quite literally tiptoed through the eerie looming of Maggie's probable death, and none of us have yet to say, "Man, I wish we could go back to that time Maggie almost died." Our miracle came from the least likely location no one would have dared to visit as a volunteer. How wild that such a space of heartache, fear, and grief—filled with death—gave way for the miracle of life?

Revisiting the Nativity scene, I implore you to fast-forward thirty-three years when this little baby from the itchy, dirty hay grew into the God-man, showing up for the least of these and rebuking anything done outside of love. Christ's earthly ministry was coming to a close at thirty-three years old, yet it ended on the climax to top all finales. He would save mankind in a two-fold process that required his life to give others life. Before resurrecting to save us from our sins, he died for them. Like the beginning of a flower, he was tucked away only to burst through the dirt of despair with a promise that our thorns, while tangled, will never consume us.

Steadfast in his nature, God created an unconventional route to growth, paving death as the gateway to life. But before saving the world, he sent his Son on the scene in a place no one else would dare make their beginnings. And while most of us will never return to our sore-thumb places, Christ gently promises us, "If I had to do it all over again, I'd start in that itchy bed of hay. I'd let my first breath inhale the stench of animals and sweat. I would grant my little body the heavy ability to soak up the fear in the room as Mary and Joseph questioned how to raise me, the God swaddled in vulnerability. And I would stick around on sinful earth to show up for a beating and crucifixion, an unjust death, to give life to you. You are worth being healed, no matter where I have to go. No matter what I have to endure. No matter what you have done."

Everyday Application:

1. If you dodged the question earlier in the chapter, it's back: are there places you have visited that your brain never wants to re-map? (I encourage you to call them out or write them down.) Why do these places hold such heartache?

2. When you think about what each individual in the Nativity scene lost to welcome Christ, who/what do you resonate with most? Looking at your map of bad memories, where do you see that loss has been worth the gain?

3. I find great comfort in knowing "You are worth being healed," but I want you to fill in the blank with the place God shows up most for you: "God says I'm worth being _____."

4. Don't stop by filling in one blank. In my own life, I must include, "God says I am worth being healed, celebrated, forgiven, adored, etc." What can you add to your list?

Prayer Closet Thought:

When you process the places you would rather not revisit, people will come to mind. Like me, maybe you made a mistake and tore apart a friendship. Perhaps the roles are reversed for your landscape, and someone destroyed you. In the face of grave mistakes is a life-giving time to discover if amends are possible. After all, we often must surrender our pride and even our tattered feelings to bridge the gap from harbored hurt to hope. Is there someone you need to call and ask for forgiveness? Is there someone you need to dig deep and find space to forgive, unearthing all bitterness and malice? I'm not suggesting that we should run headlong back into dangerous or manipulative relationships, but for the sake of God's kindness, where can you actively seek his restoration in unwanted places?

5

Goodness Remains

"HEY, PEYTON. HOW ARE YOU?"

"Hey! I'm doing good."

"It's *well*—not 'good,'" Mom gently chides post-conversation. "You are doing *well*."

Insert Peyton's second-grade attitude: "Okay, Mom. I'm doing *well*."

"Hey, Mom! I've took that and—"

"It's I *have taken*, not 'have took.' It's either I *have taken*, or I *took*."

Insert third-grade attitude: "Fine, Mom. I *took*."

When your mom is a veteran reading teacher with all sorts of graduate diplomas to back her preaching, you catch on to grammar rules at a remarkably young age. (You don't question the authority, either. You just quietly sit on the front row pew of her sermons and only "Amen" when she corrects you.)

Often, I absorbed this knowledge by a strong maternal force known as "I got stuck in the car with Mom today and had no energy left to fight a list of speech rules." On the other hand, Mom was rearing and ready for the opportunity to teach an extra lesson on the art of speaking:

"You *have seen*—not 'saw.' It's you *have seen*."

Insert Peyton's fourth-grade attitude: "Ugh, Mom! I. *Have. Seen*."

"You *saw*—not 'seen'. It's you *saw*."

Insert Peyton's fifth-grade attitude: "I was just trying to tell you a story, Mom. But I *saw*. Happy now?"

"Hi! Could we speak with Peyton?"

"This is her!"

"It's *she*, baby. You always say, 'This is *she*,'" Mom whispers while I'm on the phone.

Over and over, I remember these little lectures hosted at the kitchen counter, the kitchen table, the kitchen doorway—any location that simultaneously housed my mother and my improper speech patterns.

Eventually, I learned not to resist these broken-record lessons. After all, if I learned the rules and applied them, the lectures would end. So, once I embraced the repetition of the rules, they took on a more concrete role, plastering themselves onto my brain. These regulations were stuck to stay forever, molding the lie that goodness was temporary and always hinging on my performance. I'd never admit it to Mom, but these little rules quickly became a teeny-tiny ego boost for me too:

"How are you, Peyton?" a rich but nice lady asks me in the high school gym bathroom.

Remember, Peyton. It's well. *You are doing* well.

"I'm doing well. How are you?"

"Ah, it's so nice to hear people use proper grammar," she shrieks through bright pink lipstick. "I need to work on saying 'well' too!"

You did good, Peyton. Nice job.

Rules that suspend all of humanity—from subject/verb agreement to more extensive rules concerning legalities—were safe guarantees for a timid, unsure young girl. These all-encompassing regulations were easy to identify and check off at the end of each day. They meant I could promise by the time the sun settled behind the pine trees, I had done something right, no matter how simple or easy:

Said "I'm doing well" instead of "I'm doing good"? Simple enough. Check.

Said "I have taken" instead of "I have took"? Not a problem. Check.

Didn't physically harm anyone. Easy (most days). Check, check.

I learned to love the sharp distinction I recognized between "I'm doing good" and "I'm doing well," between black and white, between Peyton is wrong and Peyton is right. It became the easiest self-evaluation form I could ever fill out, the most accessible self-perception tool available. Besides, if you mirror my relationship with rules, you understand lists as instant endorphins to kickstart the day's needed accomplishments.

But accomplishments don't always look as simple as a checked box and a gold star. Life presents lots of not-so-shiny gray spaces for you to navigate, and when the answers aren't as simple as "I have taken" or "I took," you don't know which path to take. Then, the age-old question fills the hollow halls of your brain: what do I do now?

Before discovering answers, we tend to grow fidgety and anxious because we can't ascertain the next step forward. We don't mind putting in the work to get from point A to B, but if we don't know where point B is, we feel there is nothing hands-on that we contribute to the process.

If you're like me, when you're fidgety and anxious, you're also whiny, moody, and in a constant state of exhaustion. And when I'm exhausted, I get overwhelmed with the simplest, most basic tasks. Once I'm overwhelmed, I don't think clearly. When clear thoughts can't invade a foggy brain, my wheels spin in the same aimless direction, creating one big stand-still.

And, well, *ugh.*

Ugh is how most of us feel when we are in a season of questions, confusion, doubt, loss, etc. And these *ugh* seasons rarely feel like a place we're supposed to be in, temporary or not, because they don't feel good.

But what is "good"? How do we measure what's inherently good versus temporarily good? How do we simultaneously navigate what's good, what's right, and what's also bleak, gray, and, dare I say, tragic? And how do we define goodness when we have lost hope in perfection? In ourselves?

I could point us all to Webster, but the nostalgic side of me, the part that loves to clamor after history's most ancient beauties, prefers a primordial text that surpasses AD, BC, and time itself.

Genesis 1, the first book and first chapter of the entire Bible, uses the word "good" seven times, so I think the beginning of the beginning might be a solid place to look for the original meaning of "good."

Genesis 1:3–4 says, "And God said, 'Let there be light,' and there was light. And God saw that the light was good . . ."

So, though light itself isn't the technical definition of "good," we know that light is a good thing. If we check out the remaining six accounts of "good," we find that:

"God called the dry land Earth, and the waters that were gathered together he called Seas. And God saw that it was good" (v 10).

"The earth brought forth vegetation, plants yielding seed according to their own kinds, and trees bearing fruit in which is their seed, each according to its kind. And God saw that it was good" (v 12).

"And God made the two great lights—the greater light to rule the day and the lesser light to rule the night—and the stars. And God set them in the expanse of the heavens to give light on the earth, to rule over the day and over the night, and to separate the light from the darkness. And God saw that it was good" (v 16–18).

"So God created the great sea creatures and every living creature that moves, with which the waters swarm, according to their kinds, and every winged bird according to its kind. And God saw that it was good" (v 21).

"And God made the beasts of the earth according to their kinds and the livestock according to their kinds, and everything that creeps on the ground according to its kind. And God saw that it was good" (v 25).

"So God created man in his own image, in the image of God he created them; male and female he created them . . . And God saw everything that he had made, and behold, it was very good" (v 27, 31).

In summary, the galaxies, the water, the earth, the plants, the trees, and the animals are good. Even still, held against big, burning, beautiful, bursting balls of light, God declares people as *very* good. Why? Such favor isn't granted because humans are a brilliant, cosmic explosion of stars, but because we inhabit the more beautiful, more powerful mold that formed each spontaneous combustion by hand: the image of God. Verse 27, alone, gives us every right to believe that we are no mistake, no sheer luck, no purposeless waste of oxygen, no "whatever happens—I had it coming."

We hear this truth about being made in God's image so often in Sunday school classes, in middle school youth groups, and even in pro-life speeches, and yet, we let it slip in one ear and out the other. Or at least I do. We wear it on bright pink t-shirts, sling it over our shoulders, slapped across a purse, but we don't clothe ourselves in that truth. Or at least I don't.

However, most of us don't negate such truth as a willful act of rebellion. Consider this: humans have yet to master the art of controlling thoughts and flipping emotional switches on and off with ease. Sin and self won't let this truth safely rest on our favorite floating shelf. As much as we brave the idea that we have a firm grip on speaking kind, powerful truths to ourselves, though we cling to the shaky notion that we are calm and relaxed, we stumble too quickly.

After we experience enough life to make a wrong turn, countless times, we let shame coast us down a dreary memory lane. It makes pitstops, forces us to open the car's squeaky, rusty door, and gawk at the worst parts of us plastered across a tattered, eyesore billboard.

This unending trip drowns out any notion that a good God took the time to delicately create our innocence in the womb. Shame blocks out this beautiful picture, and after we consistently cave to sin and selfishness, shame hopes we forget that this same God invites us to repentance. Here, we can find not only forgiveness but a Spirit who will walk and talk with us and guide us through both mistakes and miracles. This God, this Spirit, calls us good, beloved, chosen, set apart, worthy, safe, "the apple of [his] eye" (Ps 17:8).

So, what happens when we don't ask for forgiveness? Where does fate leave us if we don't take a chance on God's grace? What happens when we don't tap into a freedom that releases our captive definition of our goodness? We can't accept goodness in its most honest forms; no applause is allowed for baby steps, minor victories, or any raw and natural element of life that includes massive grace yet a meager ounce of imperfection.

What happens when we stay on this gloomy tunnel's train tracks? We throw a blinder on the train's big front light, covering up the freedom that two things can be true at once:

Our bodies are both sinful and restored.

Selfish and selfless.

Scared and brave.

Scarred and healed.

Rocky and steady.

Ignorant and intelligent.

Bound and free.

Our past can be full of shame, hurt, and fear, while our future is full of grace, healing, and freedom. Our present can be all of these things at once. And such is progress. This is moving forward, accepting God's grace, and extending it to others. This is failing at giving God's grace to self and others on hard days, only for God to offer bountiful forgiveness, restoring our faith in his grace day after day.

Why is this acceptable? Because two things were true for Jesus at once too. While on earth, he was both:

Student and teacher.

Angry and righteous.

Anxious and brave.

Tired and empowered.

Starving and fulfilled.

Son and God.

Son and Spirit.

Unlike our walk on earth, his balancing act was never interrupted by sin, but he made way for two things to cohabitate in an unlikely fashion.

He could flip tables with this wild, infatuating anger that was beautiful, holy, and soul-piercing. He could sweat drops of fear as he anticipated nails ramming through his body while boldly promising, ". . . yet not my will, but yours be done" (Luke 22:42). He could feel the weight and drain of forty days without food and still tell Satan to go to hell.

He was God and Spirit. Is God and Spirit. It is vital to this intrinsic Trinity that inhabits all spaces on both sides of eternity, ensuring that there isn't a crack or cranny that we could fall into that he hasn't already filled.

※ ※ ※

Two is my favorite number. I met Jesus on March 2nd, 2008, and ever since, his loving force has anchored my meaning. Ever since that day, his love continues to outweigh the best and worst of the finite things that daily fend for my attention, feelings, and soul.

Conceivably, my obsession with the number two is a little over the top, but the Bible demonstrates crucial truths with the number two:

"They went into the ark with Noah, *two* and *two* of all flesh in which there was the breath of life" (Gen 7:15, emphasis added).

"For the Lord will pass through to strike the Egyptians, and when he sees the blood on the lintel and on the *two* doorposts, the Lord will pass over the door and will not allow the destroyer to enter your houses to strike you" (Exod 12:23, emphasis added).

"*Two* are better than one, because they have a good reward for their toil" (Eccl 4:9, emphasis added).

"But if he does not listen, take one or *two* others along with you, that every charge may be established by the evidence of *two* or three witnesses" (Matt 18:16, emphasis added).

". . . So they are no longer *two* but one flesh" (Mark 8:10, emphasis added).

From a biblical perspective, the number two means two things: division or union—and these two *don't* go hand in hand. Division and union aren't synonymous, aren't interchangeable, aren't friends. They can't cohabit, co-parent, or even coexist.

If two things can exist at once, but two things can't exist at once, what's true of us? For us? Through us? Once and for all, where can we draw a line in the sand to define goodness?

I have no resources, wit, or wisdom to answer this question; however, the heart of goodness beats in God's chest. He is goodness. Goodness and God cannot be separated, yet mankind yearns for eternity's tangible goodness on earth. Narrowing such a pure, delicate concept into a couple of words doesn't seem fair. Goodness remains near-impossible to encompass. But, then again, perhaps the beauty in not knowing is the journey it requires of us, the goodness we must seek each day.

I remain confident we were made in God's image, so we are worth investing in the fight. We are worth coming to the table every day, searching for the good, true things that fill us. We are worth admitting failure—knowing that our value hinges on a God who defeated death thousands of years ago. He whispers for eternity, "Yes, I know. You failed . . . again. But you were worth my everything two thousand years ago—and you still are."

Despite my ignorance, one unwavering truth remains steadfast: we get to step into each day knowing that what sustains us is never our ability to hold up the weight of the world. We will never owe God, or anyone else, an ounce of perfection because a heart that tries and fails on repeat is forever faithful, deemed not only human but loved by the God of all good things. The beauty of showing up to this sinful life day in and day out—bloody nose, scraped knees, and all—is discovering that trying at love is worth facing failure.

Too often, we imitate Adam and Eve when they first sinned in the Garden of Eden. We sprint away from God, cover ourselves in whatever is available to hide our shame, and then we believe God is ready to kick us out of his kingdom. But, all along, banishment was never God's true follow-through. Yes, Adam and Eve had to leave the garden, but they didn't leave without a way back home. God provided forgiveness, grace, and mercy to restore all that Adam and Eve deemed lost forever.

Just as God called for them in the garden, willing them to show themselves as they were, he calls us to show up as who we are. However, as children of God living after Christ's resurrection, God isn't preparing an escort to lead us out of paradise amid our raw flaws. Instead, he says, "You don't have to be perfect to access my world. That's no longer a requirement. My Son took care of that. You're safe now. You can talk to me about anything, even your greatest sins."

The assurance of this truth nestles in a subtle theme weaving Genesis and the Gospels together, tucked inside the shortest sentence Jesus spoke while on earth: "Mary" (John 20:17). After Christ's resurrection, he first revealed himself to Mary Magdalene, who was visiting his tomb tucked in a beautiful garden following his crucifixion. Though Mary Magdalene didn't recognize Jesus' physical features when he first shared his resurrected body, she knew her Savior's voice. The moment he spoke her name, her soul confirmed the King was alive.

A distinct connection lies between Mary Magdelene, Eve, and gardens. Though Eve committed the first sin and destroyed her life in the Garden of Eden, God sent Christ to live and die on earth, resurrecting in glorious light and first sharing this earth-defying miracle with a sinful woman in a garden. Christ brought the prophecy full circle. He brought the garden back to life, inviting all sinners to forgiveness and fruition under its heavenly nurture.

Jesus never forgets the sinner saved by grace, nor does he demand her perfection. Instead, he calls each by name and fills our gardens with good things that never taste death. He restores what was lost, including our hearts and hopes. We have access to his glorious gifts, if only we ask.

I have a dear friend who asks prayer for the simplest things—aching ears and even twitching eyes. At first, I thought this was squirrely. Surely God had much bigger problems to handle, i.e., me. But her prayers were answered. Always. The ear stopped aching. The eye ceased twitching. Eventually, I realized this sparkly, giddy, simple sort of faith was accessible because she asked for it. She didn't cultivate such goodness on her own, but she believed God was present and concerned about her. He saw through her sin and still chose to play an active role in the ins and outs of her day-to-day life. As church lingo goes: she believed, so she received.

If God's power and grace are so easily accessible, what is good through us? Well, by ourselves, nothing. But with God? Anything.

How could this be so simple? So micro-focused yet broadly gracious? So mundane as a twitching eye? Because God is goodness. Goodness is synonymous with God. Without God, goodness ceases to exist. With God, goodness seeps into each atom of this broken world. Pieces of his radiance burst through us, even in the simplest of ways. Are we perfect like Christ? By no means. Flawed? Of course. Selfish? Often by choice. Yet, he looks at us with the same eyes of pure love that beheld the first woman who brought sin and sickness to the entire world, the biblical Pandora who opened the box to death, and yet, he still promised her, *I'll make another garden. You'll be welcome there too. But this time, the serpent will be crushed. I won't let him deceive you anymore* (Gen 3:15).

In John 5, we read the account of another iconic miracle (though not quite as illustrious as Christ's resurrection). Jesus heals the lame man lying by the Pool of Bethesda. After the healed man takes up his mat and walks free of sin and disease, the Pharisees swarm Jesus, ready to unleash the law on the biggest threat to their scapegoat ordinances: "So the Jewish leaders began harassing Jesus for breaking the Sabbath rules. But Jesus replied, 'My Father is always working, and so am I'" (John 5:14 [NLT]).

When it comes to bestowing goodness on people, Jesus knows no limits. He isn't bound by rules of the Sabbath or by Satan's schemes. He doesn't need our perfection, nor does he require pretty prayers with red bows to match. He is goodness, so goodness must follow him wherever he goes. What a glorious, golden view of the gospel. We have access to four wondrous accounts—Matthew, Mark, Luke, and John—of God scattering beauty throughout the earth through his Son.

After all, even the believing thief hanging on the cross had the most glorious ending to his story. From Eve to the thief, one truth remains steadfast: when we behold Jesus for who he is, we can't walk away without Goodness following, without Goodness flooding our hearts and bringing hope to the darkest places.

And if God strives with us always, then goodness is up ahead, already resting in the future. God surrounds our present and fills our future with himself, with goodness. Perhaps that's why we are told to not fear the things to come. Because God already embodies those spaces, and he is already prepared to bless us as we walk through them.

Does this guarantee our perfection? No. But, then again, perfection and grace can't coexist—and what a breath of relief! Christ knows the human pursuit of perfection results in exhaustion, defeat, a soul lacking infinite satisfaction. Grace, on the other hand, offers freedom to rejoice over victories in utter humility, pointing feeble fingers to the Almighty and declaring his radiance as the sole reason we survive. Meanwhile, grace overwhelms us with the daily chance to thank God that he forgives our mistakes and restores our losses. God is the only prerequisite of goodness, and with him by our side, both now and forever, what can stop love and light?

From its simplest to its most enduring forms, goodness is our future, for now and forever, because God's goodness has chosen eternity.

Everyday Application:

1. Read Genesis 1, *slowly*. After reading, write out how you would define God's goodness.

2. Which memories take the steering wheel of your shame? Are they experiences you have brought to the light through prayer, accountability, and/or Christian counseling?

3. Create your own two-things-can-be-true-at-once list. Does this list allow you to recognize areas that need work and pieces of you that God adores?

4. When you think of God's radiance, what comes to mind? Which essences of God do you see shining through in your daily life?

Prayer Closet Thought:

Goodness surrounds us, though it can often be hard to see amid life's chaos. The Holy Spirit envelops us, though it can often be hard to feel him amid life's biggest worries. Wherever you're sitting, pause. Observe the scenery. Is there goodness in the hot cup of tea you're sipping? Is there goodness as children laugh and tumble through your living room? Is there goodness as birds chirp and music plays in the distance? As your husband cooks breakfast? Is there goodness in the way people open the door for one another at the coffee shop? Or the way people of all colors and backgrounds make the simple effort to smile at one another in the grocery store? Find the goodness, and there, you will find his Spirit.

6

An Avenue for Peace

❖

REFLECTING ON JESUS' CHILDHOOD, I always imagined him carving benches and tables with his earthly dad, Joseph, or aiding his mother, Mary, by feeding goats, hauling hay, building fires for evening meals, etc. His people were oppressed not just physically but financially too. Rome had a firm, dictatorial grip on the Jewish nation's economy (or lack thereof), so I picture his day-to-day activities ruled by nothing more than acts of survival. Yet, to my heart's delight and surprise, I recently discovered that his childhood was not completely robbed of laughter and light. The Christian History Institute reveals that archaeologists have found toys and games of Christ's time similar to what we know now as jacks, hula hoops, hopscotch, and even an ancient game similar to modern-day checkers for adults. Furthermore, history leads archaeologists to believe even Jewish children had access to these games and toys, offering a glint of joy amid the brutal control of Ceasar.

Of course, technology has taken the most basic forms of entertainment and dressed their play in lights and sounds and extra gadgets. But, despite the explosion of technology, my favorite game's birthday dates back nearly a century ago, my classic selection surprising no one who knows me well. My grandmother, Bonnie, says I have always been an old soul, forsaking the ways of modern society in pursuit of life's more straightforward rhythms. I prefer the pastel green Frigidaire over any of today's sleek, stainless-steel kitchen appliances. Rod Stewart and Billie Holiday swallow most of my playlist—forget Billie Eilish or Rihanna. So perhaps my favorite board game, Clue, further confirms Bonnie's theory of my vintage sentiment.

In 1943, Clue hit the scene, a guess-who board game that sends each player on a thrilling journey to solve a murder. Players must discover clues to uncover which character is the killer, which weapon he/she used, and where the murder took place. As a kiddo binge-watching CSI by age eight, a kiddo whose first big career ambition was to be a Forensic Sculptor, I guess you can say I was fascinated with crime, with the motive behind drastic things.

I recall my interest peaking during an episode when one investigator discovers a person's tooth buried in the soot of a grandiose mansion's fireplace. This sole tooth pivoted the investigation and led detectives to the killer. The gore and guile of sin's most vicious violations never appealed to me. Still, I was glued to hard questions and subtle clues because I found purpose and satisfaction in uncovering answers, better yet, truthful answers. I found meaning in digging to the heart of why people did what they did—even if what they did was revolting, heart-shattering, or both.

To this day, a little piece of my eight-year-old self loves playing Clue. Yet, as a grown woman who has lived through much harder, tougher challenges than correctly identifying Professor Plum with the candlestick in the billiard room, I am even more driven to unearth the hearts of people. I crave to understand people's motives, especially the seemingly wrong motives, before I judge them or question God. No matter the heinous act, quiet questions creep toward the front of my mind: do they have severe childhood trauma? Is there a mental health problem altering the brain's communication with the body? Is there any chance they do not have a soul—is that possible on an earth ruled by God's spiritual kingdom?

The more life I live, the more I try to unearth my motives and why I do what I do. So, before I go any further, I must admit two truths I have found both pivotal and healing as I sleuth my way through particularly desert-like places in my walk with Christ:

Questioning why things happen—from why good things happen to bad people to why bad things happen to good people—is not a lack of faith. Rather, a righteous inquisition is a natural human response to ignorance. Ignorance humbles us into the undeniable truth that we are not in control, and at the same time, our need for answers prods us to search out the character of God. (As I like to say, if you ask questions, even questions bred from hurt and fury, that is a telltale sign your heart is on a holy pursuit. You care enough about God to understand who he is and how he operates.)

Showing up with questions laced in anger, hurt, and even pure fury will never deter God's ability to invade the thick, foggy atmosphere we are trudging through. His power has never centered on our emotions, but it has forever shown up purely because we need him. God's goodness permeates our darkest spaces, shedding light on love hidden by sin's best masquerade. What more crucial time do we need him than when we cannot understand the cruel, deceptive world surrounding us?

Even with these truths tucked safely in my satchel, I struggle against halfway faithfulness as I seek to understand God's pure aim for my soul amongst tainted things. Chasing down truth in trying times feels much like reading the eye exam chart, getting three or four lines in, and knowing full well that everything is far too blurry to press forward. Angst rises in my throat as I realize I have reached a stopping point and hit a brick wall. Pride fights a pointless battle as I admit to the doctor that I no longer know what is happening because I can't see what is unfolding. Things are too gray and smudged for me to bank on my understanding, and in a realm outside eye charts, guessing at justice, flipping the coin on who deserves mercy and grace, is not only foolish, but a brutal seizing of authority that was never ours.

When you have searched all you can and are still left clueless, or if you bypassed waiting for answers and took matters into your own feeble hands, it can be easy to look up at God and ask, "Why are you allowing this to happen? I can't see you. I can't feel you. I can't find you. What is going on, God?".

I recently poured these questions out to God when I discovered that my Little from my college sorority had passed away. This news came in the form of a five a.m. text message from another sorority sister. Though she had no specifics to offer, she wanted me to know the basics before such heavy news exploded on social media. I recall skimming through the message and then re-reading it multiple times as I took in the reality of her tragic death and felt the weight of guilt for words left unsaid. This year was the first year I had ever forgotten to tell her Happy Birthday (and her birthday came only a few short weeks before her death).

That same morning, I fell back asleep, but less than a few hours later, I was wide awake to a reality flooded with remembrances of how many times I should have paused my busy schedule to text her and ask how her newest baby girl was doing. But something else centered on me always seemed more important.

From the moment that five a.m. text sunk in, I adopted so much fear. So much shame.

So many racing thoughts.

So many memories that would sear my stomach and scar my soul while I was in the shower, scrolling through social media, and doing anything grief could invade in the slightest.

I do not share this story in pity, begging you to match my grief as you read through this gray season of mine, but for my Little's memory, I ask you to process how dark the world grew the second she left this earth. You see, to know her was to understand light, love, and pure laughter. Her presence eased the tensest, anxious rooms with an innocent warmth. You never had to question her motives—why she showed up just to say hey, why she went out of her way to have a humongous blanket monogrammed for you, why she would bear hug you out of nowhere. Her intentions were pure all the time.

She was comfortable in her skin, unafraid to sport a ponytail, t-shirt, and no makeup. A secret piece of me always envied how secure she felt with herself. Another piece of me still envies how effortless it seemed for her to love people just as they were. I cannot recall a single time I heard her say anything wrong about anyone. She loved people. She loved to love. And everyone who had known her for at least five minutes felt that same ebb and flow of kindness that followed her everywhere.

Her guttural laughter was healing; it was the sort of balm my heart needed at nineteen when the first guy I ever loved broke me into millions of little pieces. Her love for me was constant, never wavering as time passed, and we moved from one life phase to the next. She brought the most precious gift to my bridal shower and vied for her spot in line as one of the first to purchase my debut book, *Not so by Myself*. In short, my Little was a good human being, the kind of genuine, loyal person you rarely find in today's me-crazed culture.

For nearly two months, I not only carried the weight of her death, but I struggled with the question of how she died. Just like Clue, I now had to scrounge for my own resources, search through my own files, to figure out who, what, where, when, why, and how. At this time, my Little and I lived 1,400 miles from each other, so meeting up with other sorority sisters to discuss the tragedy was not an option. Time was not on my side as I had little opportunity to rearrange my work schedule, book a flight, and attend her funeral. Resources and research left me empty-handed, living so far away. Each person, each connection, each search engine dropped me off at a dead end, and all the while, my soul found no justified way to approach her closest loved ones with such a serious, possibly insensitive question of what happened.

Eventually, I discovered the answer. It was an answer I had mulled over in the back of my mind, a solution I had always twisted and turned into an impossible cause—not because it was impossible, but because I refused to accept the possibility. No, my Little would not have killed herself. Suicide? She never fit the profile for a desperate end to life. Not the girl in camo with a smile this world could never camouflage. No, not her.

But it was her. This beautiful woman with sandy brown hair and the brightest brown eyes I will ever see found solace in leaving behind her struggles—struggles I never picked up on.

With discernment and intuition rarely failing me, all I felt to blame was my laziness, my selfishness that was more focused on my routine than taking five seconds to send her a text. No surprise, this fatal discovery packed on more shame.

More racing thoughts.

More memories that made me feel less like a victim and more like the killer. I could no longer complain that I had been punched in the gut, nor could I wallow in my grief. No, not when I was questioning if my lack of showing up, my lack of being there to see this coming, was the murder weapon, a pivotal part of the problem that led to this preposterous ending.

My moment of guttural ruin had come in the form of that five a.m. text message. Such an unexpected reality hurt, but the text held a solid, sure answer. My Little had died. It was a fact I could accept without directly involving myself. Meanwhile, the "But am I to blame?" moment invaded my soul, the enemy pressing the sinister notion that I was a big, inseparable part of both cause and effect.

I've known what it's like to lose a loved one, someone who took a piece of your soul with them that you know you'll never get back. However, until this unthinkable tragedy, I had never known what it was like to feel as though I aided in the loss. I'd never seen myself as the one holding the candlestick in the billiard room, but her death changed all that.

I wasn't sure what to do with the guilt—outside cry about it. Death leaves no room for band-aids, no time for apologies. It leaves you with yourself. And what you did or didn't do.

"What am I supposed to do with this, God?" I asked. "Can you show me what you're doing here?".

"Just grieve."

It took days of tears, questions, and anger, but eventually, he spoke those few words most gently.

"Just grieve."

This answer wasn't a band-aid, nor did it resolve my guilt, but it did force me to focus on grief, taking it for all it is and isn't.

As someone who not only loves mysteries but craves all history has to offer, I dove into understanding the beginnings of the word "grief." It's a Latin term that didn't show up until around the year 1,200, but I find it fascinating that while many of us know grief as a noun, a thing we experience, grief began as a verb—to grieve. Yet, to suffer doesn't necessarily mean to cry, nor does it mean to mourn. Instead, in its most basic form, to grieve means to burden. To pick up what is heavy and carry it forward.

While my spirit joyfully clung to the redeeming act of carrying my grief forward, I can't fall short of sharing more. You see, the origin of such sorrow strives for richer soil. Grief shares a root meaning with "gravity"—not just the seriousness of a situation, but "gravity"—as in the invisible force (Force) that keeps us grounded.

So, when Jesus was whispering to me, "Just grieve," he was saying:

"Move forward, Peyton. The memories and the present hurt can all come along, but we must move forward. Your life isn't meant to stop here."

"You are grounded despite your grief, Peyton. You can feel what you need to feel, and meanwhile, I'll make sure the pain, shame, lies, and hell's most stealthy blows never uproot you. Your life doesn't stop here."

"I have grieved for you, Peyton. When I picked up the heavy burden of the cross and carried it forward, drug the splintery beams toward Golgotha's hill, you weren't just on my mind, but your burdens were on my back. I felt each of them, but you were worth every agonizing step, bloody beating, and each ounce of my deepest wounds. My life wasn't meant to stop on that hill because your soul depended on mine."

Perhaps grief is a spiritual gravity, a force used by God, to keep us rooted in truth and call us to continue growing—even when grief leaves us feeling as if we are caught in a wasteland with no signs of life or light nearby. Perhaps we are meant to keep going because God has given us value that holds weight, a merit deserving presence on earth.

Sure, we might look mangled and mauled on the surface, like the desert storm has done quite a number on us. We might feel laced in thorns or withered by the sun's relentless haze, but life holds on at the earth's core, layers deep into the things we cannot see. Why? Because grief didn't cause our Jesus to let go. Instead, it called him forward. The greatest miracle to rescue our souls required our grief and the beautiful reality that his heart always breaks for us.

Amber Ginter, a blogger and wordsmith with soul-healing words, paints this picture in a soft, powerful light when she says: "But there is beauty in the unraveling. In loose ends hanging on by threads . . . there is beauty in the breaking, and Jesus knows all about broken things. After all, He became one so we could be whole."[1]

I'm not sure I know enough about overcoming grief to offer a five-step process for quick, seamless recovery. The only thing I truly know about grief is that it's messy, that there is no perfect way for any of us to navigate the spaces it takes up in our minds and hearts. But, for those who are grieving the loss of anything—of loved ones who have died, friendships that have severed, a body torn apart—I can offer a few words of encouragement, a few tools God has graced me with, as I stumble through my grief:

God's goodness allows us the space to grieve. Just grieve. Those two words I felt the Spirit whisper over me held no antidote, no unraveled secrets of when I would actually feel better. Instead, God allowed me the space to be human. He's not afraid of our humanity. He finds our society so special that he embodied its wretchedness just to be with us in our flawed skin. Just grieve, friend.

Shaming yourself won't heal anything. Now, that's not to say that there aren't areas in a particular relationship where you could've shown more grace and love. I'll always know I should've shown up for my Little more than I did. But, sitting in that shame, carrying that burden, leaves wounds gaping, never leaving room for healing. Instead, you can honor who they were, the beauty they brought into your life by showing up for others with a grace and love like never before.

Never expect another's grief to match your own. Not all wounds heal the same way—some need stitches while others need creams. Some require bandages, while some should air out. As you move forward through your grief, don't let the enemy put you against others when they don't grieve just as you do, much less criticize you for the way you grieve.

1. Ginter, "Jesus Knew Anxiety Too," para. 23–24

Most of us will know tragedy the instant it arises, but deciphering its purpose is an overqualified tool for a person navigating new shock and grief. Instead, discovering the reason behind the hurt will likely come slowly and steadily as we heal. As you navigate your loss, remember that burdens are not designed to halt our journey. On the contrary, we are called to pick up our burdens and carry them forward, knowing that God sent his Son to join us on the journey. He sent his Son to die amid the journey, and he called his Son to resurrect on this journey so you and I would know that just as he picks up our burdens and carries them for us, he frees us of them too.

🎔 🎔 🎔

One of my favorite hymns, *Be Still, My Soul*, was created by Katharina von Schlegel, a German poet of the 18th century. Not much is known about her, but her words launched one of the most powerful songs that pressed World War II's Allied powers to carry on just centuries later.

Following WWII, veteran Virgil J. Bachman wrote a feature for his church's newsletter, sharing how life-altering this song was for him as he fought overseas. Our Saviour Lutheran Church in Port Huron, Michigan, published his sobering testimony:

> *I had probably sung 'Be Still, My Soul' many times before, but it was not until I sang it in a small stucco church in a tiny village in France during World War II that [it] became part of my life.*
>
> *The war in Europe was going badly. The news from the front was disheartening. We had suffered reverses. We were edgy, confused, and discouraged. It was at this crucial time that some Chaplain arranged a service in this quaint church somewhere in France. It seemed the roof of that little village church actually opened up as we weary, dirty, GIs blended our voices under the leadership of that Chaplain and the church's old pump organ.*
>
> *Halfway through the service it happened. Softly the organ began and we sang, 'Be still by soul, the Lord is on thy side.' How badly it was needed. It was as though the Lord was speaking to me in a very personal way. 'Bear patiently the cross of grief or pain'—the cross of war with its hardships, misery, separation and pain.*
>
> *As we began the second stanza, 'Be still my soul. Thy God doth undertake to guide the future as he hath the past,' God seemed to whisper, 'Don't give up, I'm still in command, yes, even here. I'll guide the future as I have the past.'*

The thoughts of dead and missing friends came as through a choked-up throat I sang, 'Be still my soul, though dearest friends depart . . .' Soothing, personal assurance [came] at that moment and in that spot. With renewed spirit I was able to sing the final stanza, 'Be still my soul, when change and tears are past, all safe and blessed we shall meet at last.'

Peace! Either here or in eternity.

As we left that little church, the peace I felt among the horrors of war was nothing but a gift of the Holy Spirit. God did spare me and allow me to return to my loved ones and His service and still preserves me.[2]

I'm not sure I'll always bear my cross patiently, particularly in the face of death's dismay, but what a treasure to know that God shoulders our soul's weight under such heavy burdens. What an honor to know that we can invite the past and present into the future as God allows time to heal what hurts. God doesn't command us to forget. He doesn't force joy on our weary souls. Instead, he calls us to press on so we experience nothing but peace in its rawest, most pure form. It's a peace we would never know if we didn't face the weight of fear, shame, and even death.

Because Christ gave up his home in heaven and gave up his life on earth, life is ours to live from now through eternity. What a joy to carry burdens if only to invite other weary travelers on our journey to hope.

So, whenever you hear God's Spirit prompt you to grieve, know that hurt must come along on healing's incredible voyage. It's time to press on, dear friend. Press on.

And with such a heavy but healing command, I leave you fragments of a poem I wrote less than six months before my Little's death. How odd the present sometimes knows the future. But then again, perhaps God invades our notion of time and prepares our hearts for the heavy things to come:

> . . . *If I was so good at being so good for a good Father,*
> *Shouldn't my calloused, cracked grip on life look better?*
> . . .
>
> Perhaps God doesn't send billowing smoke clouds, words on open,
> High-ceilinged walls to heal a brain, a heart, a body.
> *Maybe the enchanting*
> *Thing about such a mystical, yet solid faith is that healing comes where we*
> *Want it least.*
> Where we let failure, grace, and an unexpected place see

2. Morgan, "Then Sings My Soul," p. 105

Who we are—but not leave us as we are. *May healing and truth find me amidst*
Discomfort and unsteadiness, and may helping others be part of the mend.

Everyday Application:

1. What grief are you experiencing today? Is it the physical loss of a loved one? A friendship gone wrong? A marriage barely hanging on?

2. Have you approached grief in a way that left you frozen, unable to move forward? And how can those areas be activated, allowing you to mourn yet heal?

3. Think of three things the person you are grieving has taught you, three things you can use as you love others (and yourself).

4. Find a sticky note, scrap sheet of paper, whatever you got, and write down the message that God shares with us all: "Hey, (insert your name), just grieve today. Just grieve." Keep it in a special, quiet place, where only you'll know to look when grief hits its deepest point.

Prayer Closet Thought:

Do you need a warm, fuzzy blanket to settle into while talking with the Holy Spirit? What about a cup of coffee, hot tea, or another aesthetic? Often, we believe we must come to God feeling uncomfortable, as if that's the sacrifice that makes our prayers work. Instead, know that since the Holy Spirit is our Comforter, we are allowed to feel cozy in his presence. In light of permittable comfort, consider this: what poem of discovery and praise can you give God today? No need to master rhyme schemes or pentameters. Limericks, haikus, sonnets, it doesn't matter. Simply craft words that remind you that God empowers you to grieve so you can love well.

7

Steady Assurance

❋

HAVE YOU EVER WONDERED why the children of Israel were so, quite frankly, stupid regarding the golden calf they decided to make and worship? If you recall Exodus 32, God had called Moses to Mount Sinai so he could receive the Ten Commandments. After Moses was gone for forty days, the children of Israel decided to take matters into their own hands. They forfeited patience, no longer waiting and wondering where Moses was and what God was doing. They convinced Aaron, Moses' brother and the official high priest of the entire Israeli nation, to create a golden calf, an idol they could worship instead. "Come, make us gods who will go before us," they said. "As for this fellow Moses who brought us up out of Egypt, we don't know what has happened to him" (Exod 31:1).

While I can't determine if I am judgmental or simply rational, this story always rattles the same few thoughts around in my head:

If you made the calf with your own jewelry, why would you worship it? If you are the creator of your own god, why should it have dominion over you? How could it have control over you?

This "fellow" is the man God used to free your people from centuries of slavery. Why grow so agitated when Moses is away for a matter of days?

Did you miss God splitting the Red Sea wide open?! Can you not recall a wall of ocean beside you, dry sand under you, and freedom in front of you? Was that not enough to pledge your faith to Jehovah and Jehovah alone?

And since Moses has been your earthly access to Jehovah's guidance, instead of forgetting about him and building a golden calf, why did none of you check on him? Especially you, his brother, Aaron!

Of course, I have never made a golden calf with bangles and grown agitated with Moses, but I see an unfortunate parallel between my life perspective and the children of Israel's life perspective. While mocking their lack of faith remains effortless on this side of the gospel, I, too, struggle with the same key sins that consumed Israel in the desert: doubt, impatience, control, and selfishness.

The first time we see doubt in the Bible, it is surprisingly honorable. Before Genesis 3, Adam and Eve spent their time in the Garden of Eden believing in God's love for them and thus doubting that the Tree of Knowledge of Good and Evil was worth their time. (We often forget the likelihood that Adam and Eve walked and talked with God in Eden for years and years before making their fatal mistake.) They doubted sin's fulfillment and trusted God's goodness. God was their dear friend they looked to each day. But, of course, we all know that Genesis 3 was Adam and Eve's demise. All it took was one lie from a snake, and Adam and Eve confused the roles, reversing doubt from light to darkness for all mankind. People began trusting in sin's fulfillment and doubting God's goodness.

I believe this is where the children of Israel found themselves while melting down their finest possessions to create a false god. They had known God's love for them, had seen it in ways I'm not sure today's people ever will. Yet, they doubted God's goodness by clinging to the false hope that their sin, a golden calf, would provide instant, "better" fulfillment.

But who's to say that the children of Israel didn't believe, deep down, that God would show up for them again? What if this wasn't a complete lack of faith but a total surrender to impatience? If Aaron had forced them to drop their calf-making materials and think through God's provision, they would have grumbled but eventually admitted that God would come through for them once more. Patience would have saved the day.

Impatience is a pitfall paralleling the original sin. Just as the children of Israel didn't wait for Moses to return from Mount Sinai, Adam and Eve refused to wait for God's knowledge. Instead of walking and talking with God each day, maximizing the sweet, savoring, organic way to understand him better, they found instant gratification in biting the forbidden fruit. They banked on impatience's false promise to provide them with God's infinite wisdom.

We demand the prize without the patient refinement process, but a fallen world must teach lessons by experience. Adam and Eve could never appreciate God's goodness without understanding his forgiveness. The children of Israel could never fully rejoice in the Land of Milk and Honey without remembering the bitter roots of slavery and desolation from which God rescued them.

Why is patience awkward to grasp when the small yet steadiest piece of the soul is sure God never fails? We are desperate for control, if only because we feel aimless against a lack of control. Even when we unclench our cramping fingers and allow God to take command, the moment God doesn't answer our request when we want him to, we feel it's time to snatch matters back into our own hands. When God doesn't dispel all his secrets by day one in the Garden of Eden, the instant Moses takes too long on the mountain, right as things slip through our fingers and all confidence in God and self dissipates, we clamor after our solutions.

I, for one, have never been patient, and I blame it on my pride and need for perfection. Perfection requires that I have all my ducks in a row, and pride ensures that everyone sees my ducks are in a row. Yet, when God changes my plans and rearranges things (for my good), all of my ducks fly away. I have no way to herd them back in flawless order, and everyone can see disheveled green and brown feathers scattered over my ruins. But, if I take a shovel to the belief that my impatience hinges on pride and perfection, I must also unearth that my pride and perfection synch with selfishness.

Not only do I want things my way, but I want them my way instantly without error. This is quite a tall order for an imperfect woman living on an imperfect earth. Yet, just as Adam and Eve pursued a warped impossibility, thinking a snake had access to all of God's knowledge, Israel thought a golden calf they made could be their god. Meanwhile, I follow suit, chasing after what I want, when I want it, then wondering why my plans are a pile of rubble at my feet.

Can you relate with Adam and Eve, with the children of Israel, with me?

When you choose skepticism, doubting God's ability to master the movements of your being, what is your vice when life cracks and crumbles underneath your feet? When you try filling the holes on your own but can't prevail, what grounds you then?

Do you doubt your God-given worth as you scroll through social media and compare your life to everyone else? Meanwhile, do you turn to mindless shopping, eating disorders, or casual sex to plug the gaps of insecurities?

Are you impatient and angry with God's concept of right timing? Are you tired of the dissatisfying breadcrumbs you drop on the trail of empty bank accounts, broken relationships, and words you can't take back?

Consider control. How often were you convinced a situation was safest in your hands, only for things to end up fractured, shattered, and broken in lifeless pieces?

To preserve character, each must admit the reality of man's sinful nature. How often have you wanted what you wanted, when you wanted it, and your desperate, thoughtless pursuit for that person, place, or thing crashed and burned?

These are exhausting, worthless feats we show up for each day, believing our doubts, impatience, need for control, and selfishness will one day leave us satisfied. However, if we pause and reflect on God's unwavering nature, doubt's lies fall on deaf ears. We declare a tried-and-true confession that God's timing is best, that things are always safest in his hands, and that selfishness will never result in self-worth. Even still, when the soul's impatient kryptonite rears a deceptive head, we dive head-first into the same slow-witted cycle as the children of Israel. We make mistakes, learn from mistakes, then decide to make another golden calf.

For example, we learn never to date someone who doesn't honor God, and yet, we date him, break up with him, then walk back into his unchanged life and wonder why things ended worse the second time. We discover that God never intended for us to compare ourselves to others. Yet, we are willing slaves to the very digital profiles that leave us wishing we had that nose, tan, or figure. We discern humility as key to stepping into a leadership position in the office. Yet, we cut corners, play favorites, highlight our successes, and wonder why no one on the marketing and developing teams considers us a friend. We create idols and then wonder why they not only don't fulfill us but also leave our souls damaged.

The solution to it all: denounce doubt, practice patience, concede control, and shun selfishness. Short and straightforward per grammar's standards, but complex and rigorous in application, no? So, what does progress in these four areas look like on a realistic day?

With daily application as the focus, progress looks communal; it begs for teamwork. Yes, we each answer for our sins and are individually responsible for what we say and do, but I believe progress is so much easier when we shoulder each other's burdens.

Doubt's original roots stem from a lack of trust in each other. We often translate such skepticism into our relationship with God. When we grow comfortable with pushing a false, filtered self, abandoning people last-minute, and putting our emotions above another's needs, we teach each other that people aren't worth trusting. Thus, doubt becomes a natural response to being let down repeatedly, creating a quiet but deadly barrier against us and God's authentic design for goodness and love that brings us all together. Furthermore, we allow our impatience and selfishness to control our actions in hopes of shutting down the doubt, but all we do is dismiss whoever is in the way so we can ease our worries and take back the reins of our lives quicker. Yet, when self-induced chaos creates more catastrophes, we have the audacity to glare at God and demand why a good Father allows terrible things to happen.

Much like the Israelite community and Adam and Eve, we are often each other's demise. God gave us each other to traverse the deserts and weary seasons. We do life together to speak truth to one another. But, unfortunately, we use each other as a means to get what we want, when we want it, downplaying the sky-high wreckage we leave behind for others to scale.

Paul dealt with this same hardship while ministering to the church of Corinth. Indeed, if Paul spoke with today's vocabulary, he would have said something like: "Corinth, you're holding out on me, man." Paul was pouring his heart and soul into this church, building the foundation of Christianity in their hearts. He desperately hoped they would take part in revolutionizing the world for ages to come in the name of the gospel. Yet, they put bold faith on reserve so long as the gospel contradicted their coasting agendas.

Paul goes on to say in 2 Corinthians 6:11–12, "We have spoken freely to you, Corinthians, and opened wide our hearts to you. We are not withholding our affection from you, but you are withholding yours from us."

If the fear of 2020 and pure hostility of 2021 taught me one thing, brotherly love is waning. We stretch our vulnerability only as far as it must go to recruit hashtags and followers, but when a human being in front of us needs our honesty, we choose lies to shield our comfort. We attend the wedding because, well, it's a party. There are glowsticks, sparklers, and hashtags to ignite our online presence. Still, the moment the newlyweds battle infertility, we tiptoe away from their hardships and deny that even the grieving ones deserve to be celebrated for living through an impossibly heart-aching time. We feed the hungry and clothe the naked so long as we can check our community service box and keep a six-foot distance from them, shielding our health above their hearts.

We possess the potential to create a global community but have chosen to band together on no common ground outside fighting for ourselves and what we think—never mind what God says. Meanwhile, we open floodgates of permission for all political leaders and social media influencers to act as our Aaron, Moses' brother. We idolize those with the spotlight or decent title and allow their "leadership" to condone whatever we do to each other.

And dear reader, this reckless, tense pursuit to win arguments must cease. Now. But it only stops when each of us lives a life reflecting that someone else is more important than our wants, our timeline, and our need for instant answers and gratification. Self-worship only withers when God's direction takes root in each of us, and we choose to walk hand in hand through seas meant to consume us that are now split wide open as the route to freedom and wholeness. We will never have all of the answers. Patience will remain a droning practice on earth. Doubt will creep up in even the most joyous seasons. Selfishness will forever tear after our hearts on this side of heaven. Yes, these things are inevitable, but they aren't invincible.

I give credence to God for sending the children of Israel through the wilderness together. Each had thousands of brothers and sisters who walked the same path and trusted the same God to lead them home. Today, God has given us each other as weapons against the enemies of doubt, impatience, control, and selfishness. Of course, we never boast Centurion garb or stash iron weaponry in our purses, but we are faithful women for Christ, true warriors, when we:

Relinquish false images we portray on social media, instead, posting authentic images and good thoughts with noble intentions to encourage others—not invoke jealousy in the masses.

Put aside our schedules to reach out to a friend who's not in a healthy place and whisper, "I love you, and I'm going to sit in this fire with you until these open wounds are nothing but light pink scars."

Quit pretending we can juggle so many roles without letting pieces of our souls take the brunt of it all. (You can't be a superhero wife, soccer mom, Junior Service League president, volleyball coach, and Bible study leader all at once.) Rest in the freeing humility that we can't carry these things ourselves.

Replace our impatience with honoring actions. Are you waiting on a dreaded doctor's appointment? Is it consuming your mind? Take a walk each day and talk it through with God. Give him space to pave a healing journey—no need to cut corners when God is restoring the body and soul.

All too easily, we sweep past service for the sake of a simple "I'll pray for you" while neglecting to recall the person later that evening. However, some of us remember; we even jot the names down in our prayer journal. We whisper their names, break for their hearts, and beg, "God, please be with them." But perhaps we should challenge a few stagnant words in these typical dialogues. Though noble, these catchphrases lack action. Maybe God wants us to offer ourselves: "God, give me a way to be with them."

While in heaven, Jesus never looked at the Father and lazily threw around a "Dad, be with them." Instead, over and over, millennia after millennia, Jesus pleaded, "I'll be with them. Just tell me when You're ready. It's my calling, destiny, to be with them among the ruins of sin and shame. I'll go. I'll be the sacrifice. Just make the way."

Abiding with others, building community, and tearing down walls of doubt require good head and heart space. We can't pick up anyone else's burdens until we have taken time to drop our calf-making materials, reaffirm God's omniscience, and sit in the freedom of his grace. Our hands will be too full, our hearts too fretful. Dear reader, we owe each other the honor of letting God lead.

Nearly fifteen years ago, I overheard a high school friend's mom say, "Just you wait. One day, these girls will rule the world." She was talking about her daughter, me, and our group of girlfriends who loved each other so well. I don't think she realized that I not only heard what she said, but I would never forget what she said, even though my juvenile thinking couldn't comprehend the weight of her words until ages later.

Yes, my little group of high school friends and I were smart, funny, and talented, but I think this mom knew we would "rule" the world because we knew we couldn't rule anything without each other. We were an inseparable bunch, humbly dependent on each other. Yes, time has toted us states away. But if you asked me who taught me what joy is, I'd tell you it was Jenna. If you asked me who taught me that boys would never fix my heart, I'd say it was Angelina. If you asked who taught me to be kind for kindness' sake, I'd point you to Bethany. If you asked who taught me to be bold, to speak truth to the face of lies, I'd tell you it was Ali. If you asked me who taught me that laughter is God's medicine for man, I'd say it was Joscelyn.

I think we would "rule" the world because the world can only submit to peace and a proper, steady rhythm when Love rules, when people admit that self holds no merit sitting at an empty table, when people call out each other's strengths and quietly show up to support each other in weaknesses.

Life isn't about our frets, accomplishments, and needs. Rather, life is about discovering that what never wanes is denying sin's fulfillment and grasping God's selflessness. What never gets old is remaining loyal and kind in the chaos when all we want is answers. What never gets old is discovering the freedom we only hold dear when we let go of the impossible feat of herding the ducks flapping around our ponds.

Ancient days still proclaim that time's greatest epic is man discovering that Jesus remains so iconic, not just among believers but by history itself, because his selflessness allows people to remember others but forget their sins in the light of his forgiveness. He was, is, and forever will be the unchanging, passionate revolutionary.

Everyday Application:

1. Have you, too, wondered why the children of Israel seemed to consistently forget or, rather, negate God's countless miracles? Either way, how often do we forget how far he has brought us as we worry about the future, questioning whether or not he is sovereign over our hearts and souls and every detail?

2. Who has God placed in your life to weather the storms alongside you? Notice how intricately God bonded the two of you, whether over mutual experiences, traumas, or even a similar faith story. Stop and thank your friend for their faithfulness, and thank God for bringing the two of you together.

3. Reading through the list of four ways to identify a warrior for Christ, which area(s) do you struggle with most? In humility, take these struggles to God and allow him to work out the kinks in your daily walk.

4. What does it mean that God is "the unchanging, passionate revolutionary"?

Prayer Closet Thought:

Words are power. It doesn't take much living for us to recognize the medicinal calm or destructive punch they pack. At a young age, we master name-calling. In middle school, we become queens of gossip, and by our adult years, we've learned to continue molding and shaping these sinful tactics as weapons against anyone who threatens to hurt us first. However, recall the kind words and encouragement you have received from others— maybe from your professor, boss, or church leader. How did those words make you feel? Confident? Worthwhile? Visible? Just as my friend's mom so graciously complimented us years ago, her words a sort of boost of hope and life that would follow me over a decade later, you have the same opportunity to bolster others with love and encouragement. Christ calls us to honor others in the same way we want to be recognized by people. Take some time in prayer to find simple ways to build others up.

Compliment someone's outfit at the grocery store. Give a shoutout to a coworker in the big meeting with the boss when you have a chance to highlight their accomplishments. Celebrate your kiddos when they go the extra mile with house chores, doing more than was asked with a humble spirit.

Words are powerful. Let's allow God to use that power for his good and glory.

8

Forged and True

MY ENDEAVOR TO DENY perfection is eternal, a daily task to uproot the embedded weight of assuming I can master the day without error. Aware this is an impossible feat, I faithfully show up for the same miserable, failed cycle. I must whisper that grace and perfection can't coexist, or else I lose spiritual sanity. After all, only one can win out. The first offers freedom, and the other detonates shame. Perfection prioritizes the enemy's lies, and grace boasts a kind God. Paul reminds us in Ephesians 2:6–7, "And God raised us up with Christ and seated us with him in the heavenly realms in Christ Jesus, in order that in the coming ages he might show the incomparable riches of his grace, expressed in his kindness to us in Christ Jesus."

However, when shame snags the upper hand, and the enemy has a field day with my mind, I dive too deeply into the past. Not my past, though my most morose moments are frozen in unchangeable time, but rather, the broader history of mankind. If I engulf myself in the past, preferably centuries behind the here and now, Peyton hasn't inhabited time and space yet. Peyton's mistakes aren't real yet. Peyton's future isn't rocky as a result of any present-day failings. In a world buried centuries behind me, I'm free of my existence.

As a means of grappling after this temporary escape, I'm an avid historical fiction reader. Reading is a sneaky vice appearing rigorous yet pleasant, but abused, it's as deadly as ecstasy. Any plot enveloping an independent woman and two rugged men vying for her affection—all based on real people who let me forget where I am and who I am—and I am addicted.

Now, I will say reading historical fiction, though spiritually distracting, does tend to divulge pivotal facts about standout women, groundbreaking females most textbooks neglect. Unearthing this sense of girl power inspires me to do big, hard things like these women:

Mileva Einstein. After reading *The Other Einstein*, I can tell you that most scholars believe the majority of Albert Einstein's physics discoveries were his wife's. Still, no one in their time would dare let a woman take such esteem in the world of academia.

Emily Warren Roebling. Since reading *The Engineer's Wife*, I can also reveal that New York City's dashing Brooklyn Bridge wasn't designed and brought to fruition by a man but by a woman.

History is a sweet, inspiring escape for my soul on the rough days, so I was fascinated to learn about the first female forgers of the 14th century. Research reveals that unlike so many other lady leaders I've read about, these women behind the anvil and heat have called me to face my present-day reality.

Essentially, forgers are blacksmiths, and while so many of us imagine big, burly men smudged in soot and soaked in sweat, women entered this forging job space and slowly made a history all their own.

These ladies, as early as the 14th century, often stepped into a forging career immediately following grief. After blacksmiths passed away, most of their wives would take over the trade, not only learning the ways of the business but forging with their own two hands.

They delved into the craft of the fire and anvil, learning that beauty quite literally comes from ash. In fact, these women often surrendered the comforts of social acceptance to pursue this trade. Amid grief and hardship, these widows were breaking ground.

Granted, women didn't invent metalworking, nor do females dominate the field today, but these early forgers found that there was a journey to honoring the rougher side of things. Admiration remains for those who show up after grief and decipher the meaning of ruins.

It is a unique hope only produced after facing heat, working through sweat and soot, and enduring the beating and breaking of ground. This hope makes way for life. Just as the forger's product only existed following a grueling refinement, just as hope only follows tragedy, grace only exists when perfection ceases. Perfection must die; we must grieve our pursuit of its impossibility for grace to be born.

To access a grace free of perfection's weight, I must face that I will:

Forget to send out an important email for work.

Let a cussword slip through my brain the moment I hop into a too-hot shower.

Grieve a broken friendship shattered by my selfishness.

Step out of a doctor's office in fear of live-or-die test results.

Inwardly rejoice when the woman I'm jealous of is walking through a challenging season.

Skip church because I'm "too tired" but hike or dine out that same day.

Whether petty or severe, intentional or forgetful, within my control or not, these are all prerequisites for receiving grace. I can't dodge my soul's season of mourning the undeniable truth that my blooper reel will live on repeat. I can't neglect that the past will creep up on the present, and the here and now will welcome uninvited seasons in my future. Why? As a finite creature, the limited conglomeration of imperfection and time confines my abilities. No amount of hiding in the past will deter the power of the present. The here and now will pull me into an unstoppable reality.

Reality will shove all life does and doesn't have to offer in my face, watching me wobble and totter through dismal seasons and shattering losses with sin offering a worthless way out. In fact, one of the enemy's favorite lies is convincing me the only way out of my tainted reality is to dodge imperfection altogether. If you can master the present, you can forgive the past and have a flawless future, right?

Satan is a sinister mouse in my pocket, conspicuously traveling everywhere I go, always available to ensure chaos following my trepidations. This miserable rodent enjoys leaning too close to my ears and whispering:

Your boss will like you more if you show up early, work late, and never forget to send those important emails. Don't worry; pause your family plans—they need this money too, don't they?

How often have you let that lousy word slip through your brain this week? Hmm? I'm sure God would respect you more if you could master all the thoughts in your mind. That's where I would put my focus if I were you.

I wonder if they found those nasty pre-cancerous cells on your cervix because of how often you've silently judged all the other women who got pregnant out of wedlock. It may be that this is God's punishment for you. Let's face it: Jesus says in Matthew 7:1, "Do not judge, or you too will be judged."

Oh, and while we're on the topic of judging, the fact that you're rejoicing in that woman's rocky marriage is probably why she never really liked you. You've got to get a grip on being a better friend. Geez, at this rate, you'll never have real friends. Which reminds me—are you just putting on a front for the "friends" you have now? Or can they see through you? I'd tighten the reins on your appearance . . . and find a way to get better sleep. You're looking rough inside and out.

And while we're on the topic of your physical wellbeing, now that you've skipped church but went on a hike, let's see if you don't end up in a paralyzing car wreck so you can never dodge church for the trail again.

The enemy uses perfection as its forging tool, but it yields no fruitful results. Perfection throws your heart in the fire and hammers it into utter lifelessness. But that's never been God's plan, forcing your soul to bear the anchor of life, each beating a pounding reminder that the world's weight rests on your fragile being.

Isaiah speaks to the abundant hope God has in store for us. Isaiah was a major prophet in the Old Testament, and most of his ministry served Israel's tribe of Judah. However, before going any further, you must recall that Judah was known for destroying devotion consistently. Judah bucked the system, paid the price, swore to return to God, then bucked the system again.

If coffee had been a household beverage in Isaiah's time, I'm confident you would never have found him drinking decaf. His go-to order would have been the house special, a light roast with three espresso shots. Or perhaps four. Isaiah spent grueling hours showing up for Judah's reckless, defiant people who required round-the-clock work. However, I recently read Isaiah 54 and noticed a softer message, a sweeter, more peaceful rhythm that doesn't match most of Judah's rebellious theme and Isaiah's broken-record warnings.

In this chapter, Isaiah shares a word from the Lord solely for barren women. This tender chapter dedicates its heart to those who have tried and failed to get pregnant. Today, it's for the women leaving the doctor's office with thick stacks of paperwork explaining why their body's the problem, why their husband's body is the problem, or why other parenting options are expensive but always a good choice. But in biblical times, millennia ago, these are the women who had to accept that they no longer served a purpose. Ancient womanhood required only one thing: to keep the family name going. Yet, the barren women of Isaiah's time couldn't honor culture's calling. In society's eyes, they were the withered grassroots of hope trampled by a purpose gone wrong.

Yet, this is a direct quote from God, a beautiful blessing sent by heaven's best orator. In Isaiah's day, given his God-appointed career as a prophet, he was one of few people in history who had the honor of hearing God's voice audibly. God was his teacher, verbally displaying the laws of love. In chapter 54, Isaiah reveals God's message to the barren women:

"'Sing, O barren woman, you who never bore a child; burst into song, shout for joy, you who were never in labor; because more are the children of the desolate woman than of her who has a husband,' says the LORD" (v 1).

This opening verse seems ironic, impossible, no? Surely the thoughts of a barren woman don't revolve around pure delight and song? Yet, Isaiah continues to reveal God's promise:

"Do not be afraid; you will not suffer shame. Do not fear disgrace; you will not be humiliated. You will forget the shame of your youth and remember no more the reproach of your widowhood. For your Maker is your husband—the LORD Almighty is his name—the Holy One of Israel is your Redeemer; he is called the God of all the earth" (v 4–5).

God's tenderness further unfolds:

"'Though the mountains be shaken and the hills be removed, yet my unfailing love for you will not be shaken nor my covenant of peace be removed,' says the LORD, who has compassion on you . . . 'In righteousness you will be established: Tyranny will be far from you; you will have nothing to fear. Terror will be far removed; it will not come near you'" (v 10, 14).

Amid such tenderness is where we see the hand of God forging a fortress of righteousness, rich with purpose and purity:

"'See, it is I who created the blacksmith who fans the coals into flame and forges a weapon fit for its work. And it is I who have created the destroyer to work havoc; no weapon forged against you will prevail, and you will refute every tongue that accuses you. This is the heritage of the servants of the LORD, and this is their vindication from me,' declares the LORD" (v 16–17).

This chapter unlocks the most reckless but beautiful love story ever told, the first King Arthur-like narrative that all the world's best knights could never compile while gathered at the round table.

God is our warrior whose chivalry, bravery, and heroism are undefeated, and because of his strength, we have the honor to live a life free of perfection. We don't have to hold back, retreating from opportunities, beating ourselves up for mistakes or inadequacies. Why? Because God has declared that despite our shortcomings and defects, or how many times we mirror Judah, he will vindicate us. He will call us righteous, good, blameless, and holy. Our purpose isn't wrapped up in who we "should" be but in who God is, now and forever.

Meanwhile, I must confess that I am no Isaiah. I'm not worthy to hear God's voice in such a loud, booming way to rescue his people. But perhaps I like to imagine that I can feel what I can't hear. I feel God whispering that perfection isn't necessary. I feel God promising that my flaws and inadequacies have never spooked him. Instead, over 2,000 years ago, they launched love most unimaginably, and in the face of my mistakes and shortcomings that his Son died for, I find myself clean, forgiven, and whole.

Again, I'm no prophetess, but I think that's what God wants you to know, too: you aren't perfect, but that was never God's requirement to access his love and hear his voice. He wants you for all you are and all you're not. God wants to take away your sin and offer you grace in exchange. He wants to sweep away your idea of perfection and hand over shiny new freedom to walk in love and not law. This is a complex concept to cling to when you're a perfectionist, yet the journey to grace begins with admitting to God that you aren't perfect, but you want to live a life forged by love.

The Church of Galatia comes to mind when I imagine how crucial love over law is. Paul was rather upset with the Galatians because they were more focused on the physical act of circumcision—becoming what society told them to be—than loving one another. Instead, they followed the law as a means to boost their pride. In chapter 6, the last chapter of the book, Paul drives home his point in verses 15 and 16 when he says: "Neither circumcision nor uncircumcision means anything; what counts is the new creation. Peace and mercy to all who follow this rule—to the Israel of God."

We are God's Israel when we deny perfection and embrace a life centered on love. We are the people who have access to hearing God's voice, just like the tribe of Judah had access through Isaiah's prophecies. God has chosen to identify us by his grace, not by what we can and cannot do. And because his grace is without flaw, we are children of the Most High.

As I mentioned several chapters back, the next practical step you can take after admitting your imperfection is to write your letter to your mistakes, insecurities, and inadequacies. It doesn't have to be a whole season's worth like mine. And it doesn't need to carry a heavy theme of shame. Instead, write your way through your burdens. Maybe there's one big screwup or one significant area in your life where you feel you're not enough.

Regardless of its theme, this is something from somewhere that you can't shake or salvage.

Trust me; I know the feeling. But as you write a letter to whichever failures or flaws press heavy, odds are, you'll hear the God of goodness whisper truths to the face of your lies. Each of us will have a slightly different response, but I firmly believe God will share one overarching message: *you are defined by Me and My goodness.*

Accepting grace won't be overnight healing to your obsession with perfection, but it will be the start of a new chapter filled with pages of opportunities that aren't afraid of ink stains and smudges. With time, you will find yourself a brazen new woman who isn't timid around the fire and anvil.

Everyday Application:

1. Take a few minutes to think through the subtle ways you distract yourself from facing your current reality (like me with historical fiction). Once you've noted one or two of these vices, decide if their origins serve a healthy purpose. If so, it's time to create a schedule or set a timer to limit these activities to enjoyable hobbies rather than spiritually draining addictions.

2. Who inspires you? Could it be a historical person like Mileva Einstein? A modern-day singer or cultural icon? What do you admire about this person? Note the root of your fascination/obsession with them. Does this person emulate godly qualities you want to mirror too? Or do this person's looks, fame, and prestige have you hooked?

3. Which mistakes, failures, or defects have you feeling unworthy? Call these out loud and command them to bow at the feet of Jesus.

4. If you ignored the initial request in chapter 3, write a letter to your mistakes, flaws, and shortcomings. You won't regret it.

Prayer Closet Thought:

Find a special place for this letter. Let it be a space that serves as a constant reminder that you will need to remind yourself to relinquish shame and embrace God's grace daily. I suggest finding a place only you and God would know to look, a near-sacred place that holds value, so on days when you aren't sure what to do with your pile of ashes, you can consciously choose to step into a space, read a letter, that holds eternal hope.

9

Purpose in Ash

✼

THOUGH MY HEART HAS A SOMBER yet gentle truth to share with you, a fireproof, secure promise for life's roughest days, it first requires that you understand how blindly headstrong, fiercely stubborn, and irrationally self-oriented I can be, so much so, I often wonder why God grants me the mercy to share his grace with you. This meaningful, lifelong graciousness surely requires I subscribe to an infallible life of purity, no? No. Instead, God's soft forgiveness prods me to accept that his friendship with me, his friendship with all of us, forever hinges on his faithfulness, not my lack thereof.

But, before I sing hallelujah over this blanket of God-ordained warmth, I truly can't avoid the cold nature of my self-inducing tragedies.

Allow me to set the scene:

At first, it crushed my little wordsmith heart when I discovered Josh loathes reading. He will not do it. Not a chapter book, not a picture book. Period. Though I tried countless times, persuading him that classics like *Beowulf* and *Macbeth* are riveting, I finally surrendered, accepting literary death for any hopes of Heathcliff-centered conversations at the dinner table.

Josh vouches for a more auditory absorption of thoughts. He listens to the audio version of the Bible, skims business articles online—if they include graphics or video content—but reading a whole book, as my Southern clan would say, ain't hap'nin. However, the plus side of this slight downer is that Josh will never read my confession: I am not fond of hiking. (And those fancy hiking boots we purchased for nearly nothing are far too big, even for my wide feet, so my toes hold no traction.)

Yes, I boldly admit this to every person who will pick up this book, but not my husband. When we were dating, I enjoyed being outside. I thrived while getting my hands dirty and dragging my "pop-up potty" through the woods. This woodsy activity became a healthy date day for us. But when my Contamination OCD peaked following COVID-19, it became difficult for me to saunter through woods filled with cigarette butts, unidentifiable soiled paper towels, and ticks—all things grossly conspicuous.

Meanwhile, Josh continues frolicking, skipping, and twirling through the woods. He is his own Paul Bunyan. Josh gets a kick out of going off-trail and checking out "the highest point in [insert state here]." He has hiked Yosemite, Pike's Peak, the Badlands, the places where there is a high probability you will stumble upon a grizzly bear or territorial ram, fall off a cliff, or all of the above. To those adventurous feats, I say, "No, thanks."

However, since I kind of like him a lot, I allowed him to drag me to Cheaha State Park last spring, the highest point in Alabama. I was *not* excited about this. I had suggested we take a picnic of fried chicken and ice cream to a quiet, relaxing spot by the Chattahoochee River, but he wanted a more thrilling weekend fix. After I pouted about this proposition for a day or two, I laced up my purple hiking boots, grabbed ample snacks, and surrendered my free will, letting him drive me to the park's welcome center.

After God parted the sea of biker gangs crowding the welcome center shack, we snagged a map that listed all of the park's trails and decided to do a few warm-up laps at several touristy spots. Then, we prepped to graduate to a longer hike. Josh said it was my turn to pick a trail, so what did I do? I pointed my finger at the one with the shortest distance, masking my disdain by saying, "The one with the lake looks real pretty."

Josh and I leashed our pups, Alfie and Daisy, added a few bottles of water to the backpack, and breezed through the first ten steps of this "real pretty" hike . . . Unfortunately, the map forgot to mention that the lake was at the very bottom of the trail; it also failed to flesh out the difficulty level for each hike. So, my attempt to skirt a seven-mile hike in substitution for a one-mile mini-adventure was an embarrassing, deathly bust.

The hike was downhill—breezy—but this was a perilous incline. It was incredibly steep, with boulders and fallen trees blanketing the entire trail. Each step required you to hang onto a limb, a clod of dirt, anything that looked stable. I strained an ankle. Josh was bleeding from the knee (and accidentally cracked my phone screen as his short pockets beat against rock). The dogs were terrified—well, actually it was just Alfie. He would tiptoe onto a rock, look at the next landing spot, and back up, his big brindle body refusing to move. On the other hand, Daisy would barrel down the unmarked path, her sausage ball body turning around to look up at us, her floppy tongue and sheepish grin mocking our angst.

We finally reached Destination At Least You're Not Dead. I threw a careless glance toward the lake that was nowhere near worth the treachery we had just faced. Silently, I choked as my pride fumbled, stumbling for a way to admit this misery was my fault. Eventually, I apologized for my big oops, but only after I realized that there was no loop-around, no other trail to get us back up the mountain to the safe confines of our car.

"Hey, quick question?" Josh posed to a kind, elderly custodian outside the lake's little restroom unit. "We just hiked down Lake Trail, and it was pretty steep. What's the best way back up?"

We were hoping for any option besides:

"Good, you don't have kids . . . the quickest way is back up the mountain."

He peered around the unit's big gray door, smiling in approval that all members of our raggedy party were above age ten. (I guess if you count dog years, Alfie and Daisy were safe.)

"So, there's no other way back up? Could we take the road?" Josh let out a miserable laugh.

"Yeah," the custodian chuckled. "It's about a three-and-a-half-mile walk—all uphill."

Josh placed the pressure back on me: "Which way you wanna go? I don't care."

I weighed both options, neither serving as a big win. Option one: we could attempt to climb back up the mountain full of rocks and fallen trees. This option would only be a one-mile ordeal, but there was a slight chance we would perish. Option two: we could take the main road. We likely wouldn't die trying to scale rocks and trees, as this route would be smooth, paved the whole way up. But it was still a long hike on a constant incline.

My tiny calves screamed in protest when I decided, "Let's try the road . . . I don't think the dogs would make it back up the trail." (And by "dogs," I meant me.)

Off we went, our tired, defeated, and scratched-up crew. We looped around to the other side of the water, where the intelligent people had driven down to the lake and parked their cars to go fishing and swimming.

At first, the main road had a grassy sidewalk area that fit all four of us just fine.

Not too bad. We can manage this for three-and-a-half miles, I told myself. *We can't manage this for three-in-a-half miles,* I told myself five steps later.

By now, my legs were much heavier, my brain whinier than when this woodsy fiasco began. After the little patch of grassy sidewalk by the road ran out and we were forced to traipse on actual cement, I no longer agreed with my own decision. Not to mention, we looked like hitchhiking hobos to all who drove by. Not exactly your Christmas-card family.

Only a quarter of a mile into this leg of the journey, Josh noticed a powerline trail that had recently been bush hogged. Ditches of dried clay and ragtag field grass decorated the path, but Josh was sure this was the road to Canaan.

"Powerline trails are always cleared, and if you look," he pointed to the sky. "You can see the powerline run up the mountain where our car is."

"Okay," was all I could offer aloud to continue masking my "Whatever, this whole thing is stupid," state.

Josh led the way with the dogs, promising the trail wasn't anything tumultuous.

I stood in the ditch, huffing and puffing, scolding myself for taking the "easy" trail that turned into a death trap. I questioned why I agreed to these lackluster thrills, debating why I married someone who thinks 21st-century people are to navigate land with nothing more than powerlines.

Surprise, surprise, this powerline trail was also uphill. I drug my feet a few yards behind Josh, hoping by some minuscule chance that this last-minute plan wouldn't fail us. Another quarter of a mile into this agony fest, my initial concern was confirmed: "um, I don't think we're going to be able to do this one," Josh sighed. He pointed to the remaining powerlines hidden from our viewpoint on the road. They swooped up the side of the mountain that was a ninety-degree gradient—and nothing but boulders. "I mean, I think we could technically do this . . ."

"No!" I snapped. Turning around, my shoulders slumped toward the dirt, my head and heart defeated. There was no way out of this mess I brought on by my secret laziness—except to face the impossible feat of enduring the rocky trail once more.

Our motley crew stumbled back down the powerline trail, trudged another quarter mile back to the lake, and limped toward the base of the rocky trail. Fishermen paused, cocking their heads in confusion, wondering why we were back. I hung my head, hungry, moody, and possibly dehydrated. I had no lingering moral stamina to meet their eyes and further confirm my shame.

As we walked past the lake's welcome kiosk, Josh did the very thing I did *not* want him to do:

"Hey, quick question?" Josh asked a park ranger.

Hey, quick question? Can you stop notifying everyone here that we're the helpless idiots who can't get back up the trail? Besides, they can't do anything for us. There's no other option but to scale the rocky mountain.

"We just came down the Lake Trail, and it was pretty steep," Josh went on. "We tried to take the road, and that didn't work out either. Is there anyone here who could let us ride with them back up the mountain?"

To my glorious surprise, the park ranger nodded, radioed a buddy, and in less than a minute, one of his park ranger friends told us to hop in the back of his beat-up white truck.

"I've got one male, one female, and two dogs," the park ranger radioed to the entire park as if Alabama had commenced a state-wide rescue party. We collapsed in the back of the truck, wedging ourselves in-between ladders, shovels, and toolboxes.

The fishermen gave us one final look of confusion as the truck drove toward the main road.

Shortly after, another ranger's truck pulled onto the road, following behind us. "You didn't make it, huh?!" he bellow-laughed, hanging his head out the window. It was the sweet custodian Josh first Q&A-ed.

"Nah, man! We couldn't do it!" Josh hollered back.

We did our not-so victorious wave to the custodian as the dogs soaked up the sun, floppy tongues sporting big, slobbery smiles of thanks.

Our escort pulled up to the parking lot and dropped us off. After sharing one-million thanks, we piled into the car and called it a day.

While we were waiting for the park ranger to pick us up, another park ranger had told Josh they recently rescued a family off Lake Trail. A mother and her two sons started on the trail late one evening, and after it got dark, they couldn't find their way back to camp. It was a late-night scare for everyone in the park.

Guess it's a good thing Josh asked for help, I admitted (but only to myself).

If you resemble me in the slightest, you've never been one to ask for help. As a self-proclaimed perfectionist, asking for help is admitting failure. It means I couldn't finish the job, or my approach was wrong all along.

Several years ago, I grew agitated asking God for help on such a consistent basis. Every morning, every night, I would need forgiveness for cyclic sins. Every sunrise, every moonlight, I would confess that I fell into the same trap of not bridling my tongue, listening to myself instead of the omniscient One, etc.

Such agitation seems rightly off-kilter. It's normal, even healthy, for people to rejoice over a gift, one in mint condition without sly monthly payments buried in microscopic print. God hands me heaven, free of charge, in exchange for my flaws. The deal of all glorious deals. Yet, his free gift of goodness reflected my lack thereof. The more he forgave me, the harder time I had forgiving myself. Receiving forgiveness felt like I was dropping off sin but taking shame home. "I can't pay you back for what you've done for me," I huffed at him.

But that's Peyton Garland: a woman who privately squirms at the untainted beauty of God, a God who birthed perfection and its very essence at a mere thought but never once asks for such an impossible standard of his children in return. Meanwhile, Peyton persists on her squeamish path because she remains frustrated at her inability to compensate for his glory. Peyton will share his unmatchable loveliness on the page. Still, away from word counts and headliners, when the laptop is closed and no deadlines remain, when SEO keywords, or browser pushes don't vie for her attention, she wrestles with the very truths she preaches to others.

While a friend can surprise Peyton with a batch of warm, fresh cookies, she can return the favor by gifting her friend with the most aesthetic cup of coffee on a wintry Colorado day. When a friend drops off bags of treats for Peyton's tyrannical dogs, she can hold onto any packages left at her friend's door while she is on vacation. But there's no tit-for-tat with God. He gives her everything and asks for nothing tangible in return, only a heart of gratitude for his sacrifice. He is so marvelous at maintaining perfection that she will forever be indebted to his kindness. Peyton will forever be not enough, yet is loved unequivocally by the God of the galaxies. Granted, it's not that she loathes his love; instead, she is frankly agitated with her inability to pay back her best friend who saved the world.

Most people can work through their mess-ups and graciously accept God's forgiveness through it all. Meanwhile, I'm stomping my feet and telling God he should have provided more sustainable, dependable resources than this frail body and overloaded brain. Yet, with God, there is no such thing as pulling my weight while he pulls his. There is no meeting the Maker halfway, no matching his abilities and stellar performance. He carries it all and only requires that I follow behind him.

Over time, I have trained my spirit to no longer monitor the emotions and rhetoric of my prayers, even huffy-puffy ones of gratitude laced in frustration. Thankfully, the Throne of Grace doesn't require censorship. Scripture has yet to divulge the necessity of scattering rose petals and showering glitter on the floors of souls to have prayers heard. Grace only activates through vulnerability, from full exposure to the human heart's worst parts. After Jesus faced all sin and hell on the cross to simply hear our voices, I daresay there is nothing in a raw, real prayer from his child that would ever turn him away.

In the meantime, it's dire to discover a diagnosis for this pouting spiritual ailment of mine, this relentless jealousy of God's, well, godliness. Yet, conclusive results require little testing. The answer? Pride. When we allow pride to lead our mindset, thwarting our purpose, we shun our humanity and believe we can handle everything independently. In this sinful interval, when we falter and need God's forgiveness, we begrudgingly accept that we will never master life, let alone one day, without him. Though I believe God's goodness accepts our begrudging prayers, this cycle of frustrated forgiveness leaves our souls exhausted.

We will resort to anger until we put our pride to rest and find joy in God's forgiveness amid our flaws. Anger will control and quietly manipulate our thoughts, words, actions, hearts, and minds. Regardless of our constant efforts to perfect performance, we are steered toward big mistakes when anger serves as the rudder. Besides Jesus flipping tables in the temple with a righteous fury fed by hypocrites defiling the Father's house, I have yet to witness a healthy outcome from humans who attempt a reverent juggle of this explosive emotion's fiery effects.

When I ponder biblical heroes who surrendered their pride, those who had a right to an exhaustive, heavy dose of anger, I think of Job, the Old Testament icon. We place Job on a spiritual pedestal as an example of patience and endurance, but none of us would volunteer for his life. At least I know I wouldn't. This extensive hands-on training with humility, friends full of awful advice, boils, and the like—well, you won't find me scouring the town's sign-up sheet for this position.

Most of us know Job had all he wanted, and then some, in the opening scene of his story: happy, healthy children, a solid marriage, a core group of friends, a prestigious career, a plethora of cattle, sustainable land, dependable workers. There wasn't much more he could ask for in his ancient day, which offers a question: what was his prayer life like? Was it so rich, faithful, and humble that God continued to provide for Job on such an unimaginable level? Or did Job bypass requests and instantly launch into thanksgiving for an infinite list of good things God bestowed on his life?

I assume Job didn't have to pray for too many spiritual tools. For patience? What was he waiting on? He had everything he wanted, then and there. For endurance? What valley was Job stumbling through while his whole life was a mountaintop view? For humility? He was a righteous man who earned his possessions fairly, so why need a heaping dose of humility?

Meanwhile, a perfectionist, like me, who thrives off her capabilities, offers prayers following a prideful script: "God, I am rather patient while waiting for my drive-thru coffee—and sometimes, I pay for the person's order behind me. I even drive away before they can thank me. Perhaps that counts as my humility, no? As for endurance, I always tolerate others' inability to follow rules as well as I do. But feel free to fill any gaps that I might have forgotten."

Such a weak, watered-down prayer life instills a narrow-minded perspective in one's heart. While this sense of pride offers futile sustainability, it only takes one hard season of life to knock pride down, leaving the soul resourceless. After all, pride has proven itself to be a cunning sustainer for so long that the heart never thought to put any extra tools in the toolbelt for treacherous days. Paralleling this spiritual downfall, when the heart assumes it has already mastered patience, endurance, and humility, a person's spirit is out of practice. Thus, pride's crash and burn splinter the foundational beams of our control, leaving us defeated. Our souls warp into a staunchly concaved shape, never breaking the surface of life-changing desperation for holiness found outside our mess, outside ourselves, apart from our rubble.

Much like Job, I must sit on a pile of ash, garb myself in itchy sackcloth, and tell everyone with puny advice to leave my spiritually naked presence. However, though Job and I share in the ruins, my pride turns failure into shame. Job clawed his way out of shame's realm. Eventually, he dusted off the ash and confidently told his wife never to mock their God. He found a gem of God's nature only accessed when we have no one left to turn to except him. A humble, God-driven heart sees ash as a blank blueprint, a launching pad for the proper way to see self, creating room for a more beautiful, aligned, just, picture of God.

Alas, these differing perceptions, mine versus Job's, meet head-on when trouble arises, when we stop long enough to realize we are surrounded by a season of once lush land now charred. Following this detrimental discovery, we have a crucial choice: continue to believe we can fix a massive mess on our own, or choose the humble path we find at the end of Job's story:

"I know that You can do all things, and that no purpose of Yours can be thwarted. I had heard of You by the hearing of the ear, but now my eye sees You, therefore I despise myself, and repent in dush and ashes" (Job 42:2, 5–6).

God's unstoppable plan won't leave us in ashes, in an unpredictable pile of ruins. Yet, if God's plan is for me to realize that he is the Sustainer of all things good, of all (my) accomplishments, all (my) patience, all (my) endurance, all (my) humility, then I daresay it makes sense that he drives people to a place where they cannot sustain the good things in their lives. The "my" is no longer, well, mine.

When I weigh out how humiliating, frustrating, and tiring it can be to land on my hind end, knowing I have self to blame, then a big piece of me is willing to repent. There is a warranted, unavoidable willingness for me to step back and say, "Okay, God. I'm here. In this desert, disgusted with the mess I made. Show me how to humble my heart, and then I will worry about the existential tragedy."

God's end goal for us isn't exile, nor does God enjoy watching us suffer. However, his sole purpose is to curate our hearts into humble, willing vessels that beat for others over self. And if that requires a season of sackcloth in exchange for internal wholeness, then now is the time to lay down our weapons of perfection and confidence and surrender to goodness created by God.

I imagine God as the custodian Josh and I waved to while on our embarrassing lift back to the car. God laughs in the warmest way, gently saying, "Hey, you didn't make it? There's a better way out than what you had planned."

If I can discover a purpose that outbids my limited abilities, I can bypass wallowing in the ashes and choose to sit amid my failures. I can activate a desire for the hope that craves something more freeing and secure than my performance. And if I render performance useless in the eyes of grace, perhaps that is the water in the wilderness, the beauty in ash.

Everyday Application:

1. As you examine relationships and achievements in your life, identify the one place pride most easily rears its head. Why do you think pride chooses this area to thrive?

2. Once you have identified this area of pride, highlight a big pile of ash you have faced because of it. Did you try to handle the work project alone and fail to gain the client? Did you think you could fix your marriage, but you still haven't fixed your spouse? Or even yourself? What must you begrudgingly admit to God that you can't handle yourself?

3. Whatever it is you can't handle alone, practice taking it to God morning and night. This prayer doesn't have to be elaborate or poetic. Simply bring him this problem—regardless of how you feel—and allow him to do the work you can't do on your own.

4. Morning and night, you now face your limited abilities. The enemy can use this to create shame and frustration in your heart. But rather than leave him room to crush your spirit, make a list of three to five ways handing this problem to God will grow you as a person. Will it allow you to build healthy camaraderie with your coworkers, possibly producing healthy friendships? Will stepping away from nit-picking your spouse leave more room for God's voice in their life—and yours?

Prayer Closet Thought:

Let's confess it as a group: lists are fun to make but never fun to live. Living our lists can't compete with pretty highlighters and curlicue doodles. Living our lists requires the spiritual blood, sweat, and tears of actively engaging in the most challenging parts of life. Take the list from application number four and identify practical, physical ways you can work through each part of your list. Choose one part of your list per day to actively engage, creating a simple, small, but succinct habit of allowing humility to step in for pride and God to step in for self.

10

Chains for Joy

※

OVER THE YEARS, I have cultivated a love/hate relationship with the New Testament book of Colossians. I've read its verses repeatedly, decked out each line with blue and pink highlighters, drenching its margins with stars and notes. It's a short, simple read—and unlike the Church of Galatia, Paul is applauding the Colossians—but this book holds too many verses that, once processed, force you to confirm, "Now I'm accountable for living these challenging truths."

Colossians is packed with many gut punches, too closely paralleling a boxing champion's strategy. Boxing champions tend to predict their wins, even if their confidence isn't quite arrogance, but just as they anticipate the upper hand on their opponent, they are also aware of the violent price they must pay. To receive the prize, these champions must bash their foe *and* volunteer to be pummeled:

Eyes swollen shut.

Teeth knocked out.

Abs bruised.

Ribs broken.

Brain undeniably damaged.

Trauma untreatable.

The assault gamut promises that victory will not come without the sort of price that threatens life itself.

In Peyton Garland's world, such is my heavyweight experience as I wade through Colossians. Because of Christ, I am a winner, a champion forever. The gold, gaudy belt is mine. These things I know, but so many days in this Christian life feel like I show up just to get pushed around and punched in the face until bedtime, without any promise that the bruises, broken bones, and brain damage hold merit.

These left and right-hooks fly from everywhere—from petty fender benders to unavoidable health appointments that promise blood-rushing news. I stumble in this fog of fear without full-fledged proof that I will take a win for the day, that I deserve to fall asleep with the gold belt on my pillow beside me. All while I'm fighting these hard days, the relentlessly tumultuous routine, I navigate brutal verses in Colossians:

Colossians 3:3 – "For you died, and your life is now hidden with Christ in God."

Colossians 3:13 – "Bear with each other and forgive one another if any of you has a grievance against someone. Forgive as the Lord forgave you."

Colossians 3:18 – "Wives, submit yourselves to your husbands, as is fitting in the Lord."

Colossians 4:18 – "I, Paul, write this greeting in my own hand. Remember my chains. Grace be with you."

Full disclosure regarding my humanity: there are times when I don't want to die to my desires. There are places I want to go and things I want to do that leave me on edge at the notion that God might call me elsewhere to do something different. There are plenty of people I have no desire to forgive. And when I do forgive them, a rush of angst fills my throat, the enemy trying to convince me that they never deserved a second chance. As often as I pick up Josh Garland's dirty socks, bring him toilet paper when he is stranded, and remind him that he can't leave the house without his wallet, shouldn't the submission be reversed? Clearly, I am the responsible one. And chains? I have no time for bondage, let alone the energy to carry the remembrance of another person's chains.

Yet gleaning from Ephesians and Philippians, Paul continues to emphasize his chains:

Ephesians 6:19–20 says, "Pray also for me, that whenever I speak, words may be given me so that I will fearlessly make known the mystery of the gospel, for which I am an ambassador in chains. Pray that I may declare it fearlessly, as I should."

Philippians 1:12–14 continues, "Now I want you to know, brothers and sisters, that what has happened to me has actually served to advance the gospel. As a result, it has become clear throughout the whole palace guard and to everyone else that I am in chains for Christ. And because of my chains, most of the brothers and sisters have become confident in the Lord and dare all the more to proclaim the gospel without fear."

Paul found purpose in chains, in the boxing ring of life, in the most challenging, lonely places. Furthermore, Paul had a sense of excitement, found a source of light among these chains. They even became a lifeline for those in Paul's presence: the Roman guards, prisoners in surrounding jail cells, and everyone who realized Paul found contentment suffering for his King. Paul already had salvation, already knew his final destination ended with Christ. Even still, he found eternal hope in watching his chains, his struggles, point others to Jesus. The punches, jabs, and right-hooks of life were worth it. Not because Paul wanted to boast in his own successes, but because his big, shiny belt reflected nothing other than the glory of God.

What do chains look like today? Stateside Christians are blessed to worship Christ freely, without fear of physical harm. Outside the occasional social media naysayer, most of us have little to fear in our daily walk. But perhaps a story of mine, a chain-like reflection, can resonate with you and offer insight into modern-day bondage:

As I have mentioned before, OCD is vile. It's a cruel monster, twisting and bending each truth you hold most dear. It contorts the idea of your heart's desires, but it hands the lies back to you in a convincing package that quietly whispers like a brutally broken record, *you're everything you don't want to be.* OCD bouts come and go. Some days, I can call the lies what they are—fully aware OCD is operating this sick game of Guess Who, but other days aren't quite so easy. If I forget the day's medication or experience back-to-back triggers, my weak spots are available to the enemy. He takes full advantage of maximizing my misery where it hurts most and lingers longest.

I remember one of these hard days, smushed inside an even harder week of OCD struggles. I was nestled on my couch, surrounded by blessings: my Josh, my pups, emails from dear colleagues collaborating on all sorts of God-ordained writing projects. Good things combined, this was a mighty forcefield of love, yet I still felt the nipping weight of hell on my heels. That evening, once Josh went to take a shower, I curled myself up in a ball, wishing I could wish God into making all the intrusive thoughts stop.

I'm not sure what sort of desperate prayer was spewing from my lips, but I shot out a few words that demanded I pause and recognize the gravity of what came out of my mouth:

"Give me chains for joy."

Romans 8:26 says, "Likewise the Spirit helps us in our weakness. For we do not know what to pray for as we ought, but the Spirit himself intercedes for us with groanings too deep for words."

I think this jumbled, frantic prayer of mine was the Spirit speaking directly through me:

"Give me chains for joy."

This was the little phrase that reversed my chaotic evening:

"Give me chains for joy."

It's possible that while being so engrained in Colossians, this prayer came about not by employing ardent spiritual growth but solely through repetitious reading. Meanwhile, a sure, steady side of my soul believed I had unknowingly unlocked Paul's wild reason for finding purpose in chains: he discovered joy in chains. Sometimes, we receive chains that aren't lifted as access to pleasure. Rather, they shackle our ankles and heels as an avenue to lowly places where God's hand is most undeniable. The joy for Paul came in witnessing the salvation of Rome's worst people, but without his chains, his witness would've held less breathtaking weight. Had Paul had any less joy in chains, in jail, who's to say he would have seen cells burst open and lost souls saved? Paul practiced willful joy to showcase the Holy Spirit's presence, and God calls us to do no less.

Maybe without my OCD, my ability to reach out to others and gently say, "You're okay," wouldn't pack such unshakeable force. After all, "You're okay" will never be earth-shaking prose; I'm not groundbreaking on my own. My good deeds and life-changing words aren't, in fact, life-changing without the Lifter of our heads breathing vitality into the conversations (Ps 3:3). Perhaps this is why I find joy—sweet, pure, God-striking joy—in simple messages from my digital community that read, "Because of you, I finally went to a therapist and am on medication." My chains, these vile synapses that threaten to keep me locked inside my own head, a diagnosis forever latching me to my worst enemy, are my path to God's grace and unbeatable joy.

My joy comes from a raw, honest community launched by my mental imprisonment. It doesn't welcome others to wallow in bondage; it welcomes others to find hope while in bondage. Souls aren't changed by the habitual goodness that shows up in life, in seasons that only know thriving, but by a purpose of promise that trying times offer refinement, a grueling but rewarding preparation for eternal hope. Hope will never offer an un-weathered life, but it guarantees that each sunrise is worth finding. This community leads all to say, "God is better than I thought he was. He is good and kind. All things lovely."

Lovely. When I think on this word, soft, yellow wildflowers come to mind. A breeze on the plains rushes my thoughts. Somewhere in the dis-tance, a gentle violin strings a song composed by an angel. Warmth and light fill my heart. *Lovely* seems near-perfect, most steady, so calm. Surely loveliness keeps out the wolves, blocks the devastating phone calls, and beckons only the sweetest words.

Loveliness dwindled to a hazy summer day is the willful ignorance I choose when the outside world seems too dark. Ignorance is bliss, pure magnificence, no? Often, it's an unwilling ignorance most of today's church embraces under the false label of purest guidelines. Consider this: adults and children in the Christian culture are told to stay away from, stand guard against, rated PG-13 films, especially those rated R. Nothing good can come from violence and cusswords splattered across a giant screen. Af-ter all, Philippians 4:8 says, "Finally, brothers and sisters, whatever is true, whatever is noble, whatever is right, whatever is pure, whatever is lovely, whatever is admirable—if anything is excellent or praiseworthy—think about such things."

But may I offer a counterthought to the church's idea of lovely, an unpopular opinion? While I never advocate for violence, swearing, and any sin that exploits man's carnal nature, I believe the church has twisted loveliness into my field of wildflowers, a place where only sweet music and sweet words are allowed. Those are the only things we are to think about, rebuking any sliver of a scene that doesn't depict righteousness. Yet, nobil-ity is only birthed in the face of a villain, right only exists because we see wrong for what it is, and purity only comes after a tainted soul seeks God's refinement.

We know what is admirable, excellent, and praiseworthy solely because we are aware of what is tragic and devastating. Loveliness is only found in the bravery to see sin and say that God is far more satisfying. We can't ignore the violence of a film dedicated to Holocaust survivors; we can't run from movies that depict homelessness and hunger just because their scenes aren't pretty. We can't neglect the reality of slavery and demons and abuse. It's a shame to turn our eyes from the naked, hungry, and war-stricken.

Loveliness is only lovely because it is love. And love only holds unshakeable value when it chooses to face everything maimed and still stand firm on the grounds that God prevails, people matter, and selflessness makes room for souls to mean too much for us to turn a judgmental eye.

Chains for joy. Lovely for loveliness. Loveliness for love. A high-cost but glorious resolve.

Now, I turn to you, dear reader and friend, and ask: are you ready to accept chains that lead to joy? Are you willing to accept that it isn't an exchange—that we don't get to drop life's heaviest weight as the sole way to pick up God's beauty on earth? That we will be punched, jabbed, and bruised to receive a belt that gives us no honor but gives God all the glory?

Tough questions, huh? Fumbling for the answers resembles my reluctant plowing through Colossians.

But how do we step into these tough prayers and more challenging verses? How do we embrace the valleys as access to mountain-top joy? How on earth do we find joy in chains?

Though the process is arduous, the steps are simple:

Show up for the chains. If a loved one experiences a death in their family, and you have no energy to grieve alongside them, bake your best casserole or write the most thoughtful sympathy card. Be present for gray, dark chains—even if they aren't yours, even if you feel depleted in your own life. Take note: I don't suggest pouring from an empty cup, but I encourage you to find avenues of grace you can extend when other areas of your life are overextended. Perhaps you are quietly grieving your own loss and can't take the emotional weight of holding the box of tissues for another, but you can deliver flowers, send an encouraging text, watch their kids for an afternoon. Such sacrifice and service are how people see you live out the near-excruciating parts of the gospel, the gospel that turns hardship into endurance, endurance into hope.

Weather the chains. One of the most beautiful things about God is that he calls us to weather the chains—not to spend all our time desperately searching for the key to unlock our hardship. If you've lost your job and finances are plummeting, threatening you and your family's livelihood, I encourage you to be present each day, chains and all. Apply for jobs, network, and put yourself out there in such a humbling time. And all the while, I encourage you to keep tithing, keep giving—even if all you can tithe is your time. Weathering the chains doesn't mean you perfectly navigate the situation, but you are willing to keep your eyes locked on the Son that you know is shining behind the clouds, a steady, sure Light that will be waiting until the storm passes.

Give thanks for the chains. In the middle of the chains, and even after the chains, thank God that you not only endured but survived the chains, that even if you don't understand why he did what he did, you can look back and see the ways you were present for others. You can recall the ways you gave when you had no resources to offer, the ways you found pure joy in being obedient because love and light were all you could depend on anyway. Thank God for the hard things. Thank him on repeat. When you do, you establish the reality that even the valleys let beautiful flowers bloom.

None of this seems accessible in the moment, but possibility birthed from impossibility is what makes joy so powerful. It comes in knowing that Something more loving and powerful than you is healing you day by day. And in the process of the blood clotting, scabs healing over, and scars showing off a soft pink glow, someone else has noticed that Someone else is healing you. The quiet spectators think to themselves, "This God is worth hanging onto. These chains, though treacherous, make room for light now."

Implore God to give you chains for joy. Trust me, it's not you asking for someone to hack your credit card, rear-end your new car, or get all sorts of petty with you on Facebook for the world to see. It's not asking for bad things to happen. Instead, it's asking God to show you the tricky spaces in your life that hold richer treasures than you recognize. It's simply affirming that God can use all things, even the bad, hard, tough things, as a means of joy.

After all, he's the Father, your best friend, lover, and warrior. All he wants is for you to find joy, the kind of contentment that never runs dry, even when life deals you a hand you never expected to play, a match you never signed up to fight.

Go on, give this prayer a try. I'm sure it's not your favorite prayer at this point, and maybe you aren't ready to accept the weight of these words. But try writing it on a sticky note and hiding it in a place that holds meaning in your home, where it'll show up as a soft reminder, an unexpected encourager, to cheer you on as you embrace the sort of boldness that dares God to give you chains for joy.

Write it, whisper it, or tape it on your mirror with all hurt, anger, and confusion present. Doesn't matter which emotions you show up with for this sort of prayer. God is never scared of a child he will forever lavish with love. He hasn't forgotten how tired and hungry his children were in the wilderness. He understands your half-hearted attempts at fighting human flesh. Your imperfection is the very thing that activated his love. It showed up in such a way that he gave up his one and only Son for all of mankind, just so we could not only access heaven but access the sort of joy that springs up even among the driest places.

As Paul states, ". . . fixing our eyes on Jesus, the pioneer and perfecter of faith. For the joy set before him he endured the cross, scorning its shame, and sat down at the right hand of the throne of God" (Heb 12:1–2).

What a miracle. What a God. Dare I say, what chains? What joy!

Everyday Application:

1. Compare Paul's verses that reference chains in Ephesians, Philippians, and Colossians. Where do you find joy quietly woven into these separate accounts? What one truth do they all point to?

2. What does it mean to receive joy not in exchange for chains but because of your chains?

3. What season has you feeling chained, shackled, weighed down, in a near-unbearable state? What practical, daily ways can you show up for the season, weather the season, and thank God for the season?

4. For all the joy in your life, name a time that God used true ashes to create beauty and joyful light amid the chains.

Prayer Closet Thought:

Odds are, even if you've discovered joy before, life has already presented another heavier, chalkier set of ashes for you to hold. It's almost as if you take off one set of chains to find a new set strapped to your heels. Sometimes, I'll dodge prayers about my chains because to pray about them is to call them into existence. And once they exist, I must do something with them. However, I challenge you to allow the chains to be real so you can speak the hurt aloud. Then, write down your chains, maybe on a sticky note or in a journal. Once the chains are physically visible, you have something tangible to hand over to God, something God can exchange for joy.

11

Because of Scars

⁑

BONNYE'S GRAY PIXIE CUT and wide eyes (enhanced behind thick-rimmed glasses) pull me back to my collegiate years when I earned my Spanish minor. Bonnye reminds me of a dear, tender-hearted professor who embodied an academic yet warm aesthetic well-welcomed by any student. In addition, though Bonnye spells her name with a unique phonetic combination, she shares the same name as my grandmother, Bonnie.

Threads of warmth, woven from Dr. Plumlee's joy and Maw Maw's love, synch me close to anything Bonnye says, her words like a bowl of steamy, nostalgic alphabet soup. *Ahhh*, words to savor while waiting in a cold, sterile doctor's office and facing a frigid snowstorm. Bonnye is my nurse practitioner, a brilliant, beautiful mind stepping in when my primary care doctor's schedule would otherwise push out my visit until springtime.

I was visiting with Bonnye to discuss a better strategy for reducing my headaches. For weeks, I awoke to an egregious cramping sensation pulsing at the base of my skull, just above my neck. As the sun kissed the top of the clouds to signal midday, the dull, aching cramps would spread to the crown of my head. Once night fell and fluffy snow morphed to crunchy ice, I would collapse in bed with a complete cranial crisis.

"Headaches have been the bane of our existence since prehistoric times," Bonnye explained. She not only created a few options for discovering the acute source of this pain, but she also understood the history of headaches: "Ancient hieroglyphics show paintings of people coming to the ['doctor' of their time], sticking swords in their heads."

Following this graphic thought, surface-level impulse allows extra gratitude for those who invented NSAIDs, and this modern-day miracle from God merits such thankfulness. However, dodging ice patches on my car ride home, I couldn't shake this deep feeling that the hieroglyphics meant more. Undoubtedly, the Egyptians felt led to share something richer than their strife with brain cramps. While staying hydrated, eating foods rich with unprocessed carbs and fats, and actively resting all counteract many of Team Headache's greatest pains, this picture of stabbing oneself in the head seems wilder, more desperate. It's as if this story etched in stone begged to share a more meaningful message for all of time to paint, carve, write down, explain, and seek peace from for the next generation.

I cling to the idea that Egyptians knew the horrors of an unhinged mind, one that refuses to settle down and sync up with healthy thoughts on life. Instead, this debilitated headspace desperately chases irrational fears that gain "merit" the more you believe it best to label them the truth. These thoughts curate the one-on-one attention as a means of chipping away the soul's worth, leaving finite physicality at the mercy of a purpose near-shattered by enemy neurotransmitters. Manipulated by the greatest deceiver, these wily chemicals have turned on their friendly host. They mask the truth with a false notion that God's righteous few need little help between the heart and head. Surely, if God's glory lives within the Christ-follower's heart, the mind is only subject to life and love.

Nay, such a shallow prescription weakens the power of God waging war against Satan—a brutal but necessary battle not to secure my brain but to remind my heart it is eternally victorious and safe in the palm of God's good hands.

I am eternally victorious. This unwavering truth appears so sure, so steady, employing long-term advantage, at least from a heavenly realm. Yet, on earth, day by day and sin by sin, I feel as though the enemy wins. He tramples my desperate longing to honor my God, clouding my mind with a thick, sinister idea that I am my own worst thoughts. The lies ensue: you are everything you never wanted to be, but even darker and gloomier than you feared. Most days, I hide this well, particularly in public. But most days, when I'm all alone, I'm left feeling:

Tired. Covering the bags under my eyes with high-dollar concealer.

Half in. Trying that small group for a few weeks.

Hungry. Shoveling granola bars but forgetting to feed my soul.

Half out. Deciding that small group took too much energy.

Desolate. Empty.

Real desolate. *Real* empty.

Like the Israelites in the desert, my soul and marriage were such a roller coaster of physical and emotional anguish for several years. Yet, I internalized it well, masking my misery for all to never see. There was no middle ground between the brutal rise and sudden-drop fall in my life, but a steady, rhythmic foundation was my dream. I wanted my feet planted firm and sure, free from hoping I would meet the mark, only to crumble in quiet defeat. Even as the Bible Verse Queen, I couldn't hold onto truth long enough to catch my breath. I knew the verses, the ones promising dependable life and joy. I knew who wrote them, when they wrote them, why they wrote them. But none of my Christian-school-kid knowledge was of any aid this time.

A young, naive pilot's wife, I was stumbling through a season of loneliness I could never have anticipated. It not only interrupted my daily routine, but it destroyed every label I once used as a shield. My husband embarked on his aviation career only six months after he and I were married. But, before this sudden job swap, he was a top sales rep for the Atlanta Falcons of the NFL, which came with undeniable perks. We were invited to carnivals and parties on the stadium grounds, offered the best seats in the house at little cost, able to book a vacation the instant Josh convinced a millionaire to lock down box-office season tickets. His job created a typical nine-to-five schedule, and I depended on it. I knew when to start dinner, when to run a load of laundry, when to tell my mind, "He'll be here in a few minutes. Then these loud thoughts will quiet. Your handsome distraction is on his way home."

In this secure interval, his decision to become a pilot magically debuted—I didn't know my husband was fascinated with planes, let alone that he longed to pursue a childhood dream and fly one for three decades. But while I encouraged this endeavor because, well, I thought that's what a good wife should do, I didn't realize that my definition of "good" would turn on its head.

I personified titles and trophies before becoming a pilot's wife, morphing into a golden pinnacle of "satisfied" success. I led a life with quite the resume, one I could point to on days when I questioned whether or not I was good enough for this world (and God). Acing tests, checking boxes, and smiling on cue defined me. These surface-level checkmarks quietly consumed me. After all, it's easy to hide the lifelessness of checking boxes when most of them fulfill the Golden Rule. I ran a tight ship with a flying flag: Doing Life Right, utterly unaware that my boat was about to sink. (Later, I would discover such submersion was the only way my soul would find cleansing.)

This piloting endeavor would take away my husband, my coffee and chicken nuggets drive-thru chauffeur, the source of my laughter, the father of my dog children. Josh would be out for days, weeks, and months, leaving me to be the Mrs. of the Mr. of the house most of the time. I loathed the notion that I must lay to rest my comforts to maintain stability in a lonely home.

I hated coming home to a lonely, quiet house for days on end, but I hated even more that I didn't like my own company.

Worse than now being the one to take out the trash, take out the dogs at night, and take out the casserole before it burned, I couldn't take myself out and dump her by the side of the road. I was stuck with her, with someone I didn't like. Honestly, I was repulsed by my inner being. All the accomplishments, my oxygen for bad days, provided no peace and offered no purpose because reality demanded I not only show myself but deal with myself. Instead of lying on the couch and reveling in all my lovely, completed lists, I had to face lethal monsters I had shoved deep inside my closet, stashed way behind all the sweaters I never liked and all the gold stars I once loved.

Truth pressed, *what weight do shiny titles and glittery stars hold when you can't sit with your soul and the mere sight in the mirror leaves you unsteady?* When framed accomplishments leave you squirmy, reminding you that labels—even the noble sort—submit only finite, fleeting reprieve, what then?

As trepidation lodged thick clouds in my mind, I discovered facing monsters and mistakes was a delicate process. If you have yet to offer yourself grace for even the slightest errors, working through your demons feels like fussing over a five-course meal and only inviting Lifelessness and Try Harder to the dinner table. All the while, fine China has already shattered into millions of pieces, leaving you able to put forward nothing in exchange for, well, nothing.

Eventually, I had enough family and friends softly confirm, "You're not okay." I waged enough heartless arguments with Josh over the phone until I decided to visit a therapist's office—the last place I ever wanted to be, afraid to reveal I was the pinned-up hostility threatening my new marriage.

I was the reason I had lost too much weight and could barely hold my coffee without shaking hands spilling it everywhere. This vulnerable space forced me to leave all my checklists at the door. The only thing allowed inside this small, yoga-type atmosphere was my core, what made me tick, and what made me without any socially praised attachments.

On day one of therapy, I followed the movie script, spilling all of life's highs and lows to a kind woman with a pen and pad ready. She took less than one session to offer a meek smile and gently say: "You have OCD." A few sessions down the road, she would also discover I have Generalized Anxiety Disorder and Secondary Post-Traumatic Stress Disorder.

Worse yet, another year into our sessions, she would proclaim that OCD was likely why I always maximized performance. Checked boxes thrive in a performance-based headspace. How humbling to realize that my favorite accomplishments were catalyzed and carried out by a mental disorder. *Oof.*

However, such professional insight was undeniable. OCD is a misunderstood monster. That's not to say this is a gentle giant or a feeble mongrel, but rather, its stereotypes defuse its explosions. It's more than TV sleuth Monk's quirky personality, more than color-coordinated closets and needing a clean space. Rather, it's a complete chemical meltdown in your brain. When your frontal cortex misfires signals to the rest of your mind, your impulses and the ability to process emotions and responses escape through the fire shoot, fully aware of calamity's presence. Your body is a slave to a brain that twists your worst fears into present-day realities, promising that you mean your worst thoughts, daring you to show up for others only to remind you of the possibility of dropping the ball and causing a catastrophe.

OCD is a dark, gothic-novel tragedy—just as my life was while Josh was hundreds of miles away. Light, hope, and fantasy were snatched away without resolve or escape from the lifeless cycle. OCD promises the cure comes from performance, from showing up without flaws, outpacing, and outperforming your thoughts. It's wild and irrational. Always running, never still. OCD beckons with an impossible cleansing, but most shackled victims volunteer to face the unattainable feat. They are desperate enough to pursue the nonviable. After all, almost anything sounds like heaven when all you know is hell.

But, in therapy, spilling my soul and sipping green tea, I found freedom from my shield. I unearthed more powerful protection away from the gold and steel I had used to consolidate my best moves. I breathed better than I'd breathed in years, recognizing that I had a mental disorder. Ironic, almost uneasy, no? Surely such unavoidable gray patches would devastate the poster child for Dream Daughter-in-law. But I was head over heels for this diagnosis because it freed me from chasing after gold stars. Instead, it presented an unavoidable stain to my name that would create grace in the face of mess-ups, edifying how I could access the good God of the galaxies.

Maybe you have OCD like me, or perhaps you have your unique mental monsters to face. Nonetheless, we all battle something. Perhaps it's a daily fight with comparison, egg-shell relationships, chemotherapy, or wondering why nothing in your life works. Or you battle problems so distinctive to you that you are afraid no one would understand. I get it. I get you. And I'm with you. But even after finding resolve in my diagnosis, for several years I didn't fully understand the freedom we have from these weights.

I have read the Gospels and studied them in full detail. I know Luke was a doctor, Matthew was a tax collector, and Matthias was the 13th disciple most forget to remember. I know Zacchaeus was a wee little man, the woman at the well was an adulteress, and Nicodemus, a religious leader, straddled the fence. I know Jesus was drawn to the least of these and infuriated by those cocky in their religion. But the one thing I had never thought about, the one simple but powerful truth I had never registered, came from one typical sentence from one common sermon on one regular Sunday: "Jesus died for your sickness."

"Jesus died for your sickness!" Pastor Dean Hawk of Rock Family Church boomed through the sanctuary. He only said this one time, but it echoed in my head for days, weeks, even months.

I have heard this line, or something similar, a time or ten-million. Yet, so often, most of us neglect to understand that Jesus didn't solely die for our sins—though that is more than enough reason to adore him. Rather, he chose to die for our hurts, fears, and infirmities. When he died, he not only felt the wrath of God for our mistakes, but he felt the physical, emotional, and mental weight of every dark thing in between. He felt the hurt of divorce, the sting of being lied to, the fear that love would never be reciprocated, even my OCD. Every vile thought this mental disease has thrown at me, every sleepless night it has controlled with chaos, Jesus willingly absorbed its choking pressure. And if he felt the weight then, he beckons us to freedom from its grasp in the here and now.

He is our Savior for the work he did on the cross and through the grave, but he is our Friend who sticks closer than a brother for his work on the ground (Prov 18:24). The highs and lows, the ins and outs, the hunger, the exhaustion, the rocky relationships, and the fear of carrying mankind's burdens, he walked through those things. He found no use dawning a purple robe and passing out stickers only to those checking their boxes.

Instead, he chose to blend in, to be among the ordinary, tainted people, so when the enemy says, "You went too far. That's too much. Ugh, that's what you were diagnosed with?" Jesus can destroy his lies and whisper, "I went that far, from heaven to earth, just to understand you. That sin, that one right there? Child, I died for that one too. Do you honestly believe your sin can outmatch My resurrection? And OCD? Mm, I know how that one feels. It never gives your mind a break, does it? I remember how many sleepless nights OCD kept Me up while I was on earth. Felt like my brain had run a full marathon before dawn. But you will be okay because I have been there too."

Whether you mask your shortcomings well—behind trophies, titles, and social media's finest filters—or your biggest mistakes tumble out for family and friends and the entire internet to see, we all share common ground. We. Just. Want. That. One. Thing. To. Go. Away.

Far, far away.

Right here, right now.

No matter what.

Our desire for reprieve calls us to volatile desperation, an open, ravenous terrain where we willingly forget who we are so long as we rescue ourselves from the demon close on our heels.

Maybe your demon is OCD. Perhaps yours is loneliness as you simply request your husband be home for more than two days at a time. Perhaps it is something completely different. We each know the burden that gnaws at our soul, the thick cloud that fogs our heart and threatens the light and life we pursue. We find no purpose in naming our greatest persecutor because it announces its presence with nauseating fanfare, contaminating how we see ourselves, others, and God.

While I don't have the cure for everyone's worst days, for everyone's one thing, I can promise you that trying to cover up the hard times with more accomplishments will leave you exhausted at best, bitter and angry at worst. And, honestly, your one thing might not go away on this side of heaven; I can't say. However, I can boldly proclaim that healing is for all of us, maybe not how we would map it out, but it's guaranteed for those who look to the Great Physician.

I have been in and out of countless doctors' appointments, not just for my brain but my body too—cut here, probed there, tested everywhere. I have been cheated on, lied to, used, and emotionally manipulated. Meanwhile, I have had the church pile on shame and OCD pile on more fear. I am far too familiar with the weather hazards of life's worst seasons. I have lost my Pepa, my grandfather who would sneak my car to the auto shop and have a new tire put on, never telling my parents I had bulldozed another curb. I have grieved watching my father battle Post-traumatic Stress Disorder and Traumatic Brain Injury, being subjected to a life of pills because he chose a career of bravery, honor, and sacrifice.

I know hurt, and I am well-acquainted with loss. Grief is my pocket mouse, and pain a relentless stalker. But knowing Jesus carried the weight of all things means he also defeated them. And if he defeated them, I believe he is our go-to, the One pointing out the final destination, where peace, purpose, and steady ground welcome us home. He is the One who doesn't force you to ride the relentless rollercoaster of lifeless emotions and mandated achievements. After all, burdens bear better on his back. As the great Victor who casts your fears into the pits of hell, God calls you to stop running from your demons, turn and face them, and fearlessly declare, "You stop here. You don't belong where my God is taking me."

Jesus welcomes us into a righteous *Midsummer Night's Dream* where the end promises a satisfying resolve, a humanly impossible land of wondrous, desperate love. Still, Puck's deceiving schemes touch none. Christ offers a pure delight, an enchanting but trustworthy love without trick spells or potions. This rich, wild, unhuman pursuit for your heart means he faced and defeated death, so all you would know is life. He sacrificed all to receive our relentless burden in return.

Alas, this promise cannot guarantee that reality will always be a 1960s dreamboat. But on the flip side, your one big thing relentlessly threatening your hope now can be used by God for your good. This promise no longer requires checklists that force you to meet the mark of mankind's success. Instead, it frees you from perfection's useless game and reminds you that this is a journey. And meanwhile, others can witness your growth through this voyage, taking in the reality that you not only survived but also found peace. Then, they, too, can believe in a good God who has yet to require performance and perfection as access to a beautiful, eternal life.

I now recognize that I must live under the chronic weight of OCD, which countless prestigious doctors classify as a disorder with the potent debility of lung disease and diabetes. Now I rarely use concealer to hide the bags under my eyes. I have found subtle but beautiful solace in being human at the mouth of my biggest blunder, the biggest failure outside my control. Peaceful rhythms allow natural skin that has fought real sleepless nights and actual stress-induced breakouts to heal in the bare light of the sun, even in front of others. There is a humming, natural glow to allowing deep-rooted scars to battle impurities and discover soft healing.

These days, I actively choose to slow down, not committing to small groups or church events if I know my spirit needs to rest. I have given up backpedaling and white-lying my way through why I could not make it to the second meeting in a row. Now, I find myself a woman who gives grace to herself and others. I keep Jesus as my center priority, but I also separate serving Christ in love and showing up to check the church's boxes. Busy schedules have room for imperfection in my life. Flaws have room in my daily walk. And on days when perfection wants to win, I am an impaired yet God-empowered human who takes 100 milligrams of Zoloft to fight the lies. I am the person who talks with several therapists and still holds to the chaotic but enticing veracity that God maximizes his goodness despite my mess.

If such beauty were not so, only temporary merit could belong to the Bible's most prominent trailblazers, their heroic status dictated by performance. And if their excellence hinged on a mastered faith, would the Bible hold value? Would we ever find ourselves able to relate to Scripture?

Ponder the twelve men Jesus chose to trod out salvation's threshold: Peter cut off a man's ear to protect Jesus, and yet, he lied about knowing him a few hours later. Even still, Peter was crucified upside down for his faith, declaring he was unworthy to die in the same manner as his Lord. Matthew swindled poor people, most notably the Israelites, from their money before converting to Christianity and writing the most calculated, detailed Gospel. After Jesus had resurrected, Thomas looked him in the face and still said, "I'm not so sure. I need to see the scars first." Yet, later down the road, Thomas bravely brought Christianity to present-day India. Many scholars believe he was castrated and murdered by Hindi priests because he denied their deity, claiming the only God as Christ Jesus—the scarred yet resurrected Messiah.

Recently, I have become an avid fan of Paul's letters to the early church. Not only do these churches' haphazard mistakes make me feel a bit better about myself from time to time, but Paul's honesty assembles the most relatable literature in the New Testament following Jesus' ascension. Paul won't hide the physical danger of following Christ and the mental, emotional, and spiritual battles of devoting one's life to ministry. He is candid about his chains, backbiters, and sin's relentless threat. But he is also bold in his freedom from shame (which testifies to God's powerful mercy, given Paul's original resume highlighted hunting down and murdering Christians).

In 2 Corinthians, Paul continues tussling with the Corinth church—this body of believers has yet to master pursuing the law through love. Meanwhile, Paul reveals the law of love gives us the freedom to be human and treasure God's goodness and faithfulness despite what we do and do not bring to the table. Paul stresses to the Corinthians that regardless of what their one internal plague is, the sole demon that won't relent, the one sickness or sin that will not surrender, Jesus endured the weight of hard days as a means of raw, real empathy. Christ invites our vulnerability on the unbearable days and still hands flawed humans everlasting life in exchange:

> "Therefore, since through God's mercy we have this ministry, we do not lose heart. Rather, we have renounced secret and shameful ways; we do not use deception, nor do we distort the word of God. On the contrary, by setting forth the truth plainly we commend ourselves to everyone's conscience in the sight of God . . . For God, who said, 'Let light shine out of darkness,' made his light shine in our hearts to give us the light of the knowledge of God's glory displayed in the face of Christ. But we have this treasure in jars of clay to show that this all-surpassing power is from God and not from us. We are hard pressed on every side, but not crushed; perplexed, but not in despair; persecuted, but not abandoned; struck down, but not destroyed. We always carry around in our body the death of Jesus, so that the life of Jesus may also be revealed in our body. For we who are alive are always being given over to death for Jesus' sake, so that his life may also be revealed in our mortal body. So then, death is at work in us, but life is at work in you" (v 1–2, 6–12).

Even in despair, because of Christ's death, we only taste life.

Despite hardships that will never relent as a pilot's wife, I am no longer in the habit of begging Jesus to take away my loneliness, even my OCD. I have found purpose in my vulnerability, in a challenging, brutal honesty that keeps me humble and offers the chance to tell others they aren't alone.

I pray that we all heal, not despite our scars but through them, because of them, alongside them. May we find life as we accept grace amid the strivings, and may we each lay perfection to rest.

Everyday Application:

1. In a season of self solely striving, refusing God's aid, I often look exhausted and come off cranky toward any unfortunate victim who crosses my path. Take a few moments to reflect and notice how you present yourself when burdened with perfection.

2. Which people, goals, or material things often leave you leading your journey, curating an impossible perfection because this one pursuit seems so rewarding?

3. In what ways do you think God can handle your journey and help you reach the goal better than you can on your own? Why?

4. Are there any resources from God you have ignored as you push toward a perfect journey to reach your manmade, ideal destination? If so, what are those resources, and how can you best incorporate them into your daily life as a means of surrender?

Prayer Closet Thought:

Perhaps you don't see yourself as a perfectionist, but let me remind you: anything that consumes your thoughts, anything causing you to obsess over performance or presentation, leads to a perfectionist mindset. This, dear friends, is dangerous for the soul. As Christians, we subconsciously attempt to swap roles with God, trying to save our day without flaw and asking him to stick around if we need an extra hand. But eventually, you will come up against an obstacle or strive toward a goal that is impossible to handle independently.

Have you already been there? If so, what can you do to prevent a second crash and burn? Are you there now? If so, how can you end this lifeless routine in your life? Are you afraid you might run down this path? If so, game plan ways to actively release your one big thing over to God each day, allowing surrender to guide you as you listen to Jesus.

12

Jehovah Nissi

JOSH OFTEN SAYS, "I'M a jack of all trades and a master of none." Boy, do I relate to that! I can play the piano; I play chords with the best of them. I know all the musical theory, understand the difference between lines and spaces, and could perform arpeggios blindfolded. But I can't read classical sheet music without days of practice. I have to highlight different notes on the pages and tape the keys with marker reminders of which finger goes where. It took nearly four months for me to master Beethoven's *Fur Elise*. So, when I say I can play the piano, I can play chords today and play classical music, but I need a few months.

I am good at lots of things: playing chords, cooking casseroles, writing blog posts, wrangling dogs, etc. But if you inquire what I have mastered, I can't say. I don't know. It's not humility talking; it's pure ignorance. If I'm the master of something, I've yet to figure it out. I certainly can't make any dish that requires more than "dump these four things in a bowl and stir." I can write, but I'm not sure I write as well as others. I wrangle dogs but don't ask if I have trained them to sit, stay, and stop driving me insane.

Being human, you are never fully intact, never wholly put together, never as presentable as you wish to be. The ducks are never in a perfect row. The day will never go as planned. We will play a sharp note when we should've played a flat one, forget dinner in the oven until the smoke detector tells on us, wrangle the dogs just fine until they yank their leashes, and break a finger (personal experience with all of the above). We achieve essential satisfaction at ten things only to discover we never mastered one. Can you relate? If so, perhaps this story is for you:

Today's true tale is nestled in Exodus 17. The Israelites are still wandering the wilderness, but the only way toward the Promised Land is through the Amalekites' territory. The Amalekites were vicious, heathen rebels with a taste for blood. Even worse? They had mastered murdering their foes. They possessed the weapons, the skill, the home-field advantage. And the Israelites? Well, they were much like me with the piano. They had some swords and spears like I have my chords. The men had a good idea of war mechanics, just as my music theory skills are fair. Yet, Israel's men were only seasoned as shepherds and slaves. They weren't the Beethoven's of war. Israel was well-acquainted with defeat, assuming victory remained an intimidating impossibility.

Yet, Moses knew the enemy must fall. Sometimes, God calls us to war. And when we know who the enemy is, when we see truth should triumph, it's always our turn to suit up and press forward.

Moses mounted a plan. He asked Joshua to recruit some men to fight the Amalekites:

"Moses said to Joshua, 'Choose some of our men and go out to fight the Amalekites. Tomorrow I will stand on top of the hill with the staff of God in my hands.' So Joshua fought the Amalekites as Moses had ordered, and Moses, Aaron and Hur went to the top of the hill" (Exod 17:9–10).

One important note stands out in these short verses. Joshua instantly followed Moses' orders. There was no complaining, no what-if-ing; Joshua simply obeyed. To add to Joshua's bravery, just one verse earlier, you discover the Amalekites had already attacked Israel in verse 8. Unfortunately, round one wasn't in Israel's favor. Regardless, Joshua knew the Lord had called them to fight again. This victory over the Amalekites would require a series of obedient steps from several key players in this game:

"As long as Moses held up his hands, the Israelites were winning, but whenever he lowered his hands, the Amalekites were winning. When Moses' hands grew tired, they took a stone and put it under him and he sat on it. Aaron and Hur held his hands up—one on one side, one on the other—so that his hands remained steady til sunset. So Joshua overcame the Amalekite army with the sword" (Exod 17:11–13).

Just as Joshua didn't hesitate to obey, Moses, Aaron, and Hur acted according to God's will throughout the entire battle. Moses knew when he raised his hands with God's staff pointed heavenward, the presence of God empowered the Israelites. If he lowered his hands, the enemy stole the advantage. Now, an older man, Moses couldn't hold his hands up the entire fight. So, instead, Aaron and Hur held up his hands for him, paving the path for God's Spirit to hand Israel the final victory.

However, Moses stepped away from the crowd despite the chaos and ancient-era confetti of a miraculous win. He refused pomp and circumstance, rebuking the need for a sash, fireworks, or parade. He knew his obedience wasn't the victory; instead, it fueled the great Victor of truth to seal the triumph. Far from the fanfare, Moses got alone with the Spirit of God:

"Then the LORD said to Moses, 'Write this on a scroll as something to be remembered and make sure that Joshua hears it, because I will completely blot out the name of Amalek from under heaven.' Moses built an altar and called it The LORD is my Banner" (Exod 17:14–15).

I find this exchange between Moses and God fascinating. I imagine Moses, old and feeble, hauling rocks, moving clods of clay, making an altar for the LORD he showers in tears of gratitude. Then I picture God's Spirit absorbing Moses' humble adoration. It's a true friendship between them. Here, on this altar, Moses longs to solidify the undeniable truth that God crushes his enemies, protects his children, and goes before all who trust in his goodness. He is someone mankind can forever get behind.

Verse 15 is the first time we see this Hebrew name of God—Jehovah Nissi. Translated into English biblical text: the LORD is my Banner.

Most of us are familiar with the other names of God scattered throughout Scripture: Jehovah Jireh, Jehovah Rapha, Yahweh, Elohim, El-Shaddai, and Adonai. We hear these names in songs, in small groups, in beautiful Christmas programs packed with alliteration. In fact, if you do a quick internet search, all of these names pop up as names for God. But Jehovah Nissi? No, it doesn't have the same SEO as the others.

We only see this idea of "the LORD is my Banner" one more time throughout all Scripture, in Isaiah 49:22–23:

> "This is what the Sovereign Lord says: 'See, I will beckon to the nations, I will lift up my banner to the peoples; they will bring your sons in their arms and carry your daughters on their hips. Kings will be your foster fathers, and their queens your nursing mothers. They will bow down before you with their faces to the ground; they will lick the dust at your feet. Then you will know that I am the Lord.'"

Even after reaching the Promised Land, God's people questioned if their Lord had abandoned them. Zion was afraid he wouldn't follow through once more. Yet, God affirms his steadfast love by declaring himself their Banner (v 22). He only asks that his children get behind him as he raises families and brings the proud to their knees. God overthrows brute warriors and captors, just like the Amalekites, all to free his people. He's a banner of victory doused in eternal hope. All we have to do is let him be God.

When we allow God to be our Jehovah Nissi, three crippling prerequisites dissolve:

We no longer need all the answers. The roadmap is God's because he takes charge at the head of the line.

We no longer need to fear. God's the first one over the hill and will face the toughest parts of the battle.

We no longer need to fight for the law because God's character becomes our pursuit, our end goal, our victory.

We often believe control and comfort to be synonymous. If we can control each decision, we can navigate life easily, no matter how big or small. If we drink our spinach smoothies and go for a run each day, we escape most health problems. If we put away several hundred dollars in savings each month, the dream car is paid for in cash. If we sign the kiddos up for karate, ballet, and church camp, they won't have time to get into trouble. If we show appreciation for our spouse by making their coffee each morning before work, they will stay.

I have eaten clean—avoided red meat, processed sugars, and saturated fats—and had precancerous cells suffocate one side of my cervix.

I have had thousands of dollars stored in a savings account, but an unexpected need for tires swept it away.

Though I don't have kiddos, I have brought my hellacious dogs to parks, pet store activities, and canine-healthy events, and they remain furry gremlins.

And coffee and loyalty aren't concrete synonyms.

Control cannot equal comfort. Power isn't ours, and when we try to step into a role not meant for us, things aren't comfortable. Just as a too-small shirt pinches your underarms or rides too high on your belly, control works the same way. We want it to fit just right, but it shows up in all the wrong places in all the wrong ways.

Bad things will happen regardless of our claw-clenching control. So, when the last shoe falls, and we are the ones who swore x, y, or z wouldn't happen—because our itinerary, our bank account, our fitness plan swore it wouldn't—we wonder if God will pick up our shattered pieces. We drop the ball and break the glass, but we want him to come behind us and clean up our messes. We find out that life won't reciprocate our best efforts, that control is never controlled in human hands.

Regardless of our efforts to create a smooth-sailing life, life doesn't care. It will still invite twists, turns, and tragedies that you and I could never anticipate. But since God is at the front of the line, holding down the fort with his banner, he knows what comes next. Thus, our best interest rests in handing God the reins.

The more I try to control a person, a bank account, a situation, etc., the more anxious I feel. The ball is in my court, but I'm not always sure when to pass or score. Frankly, I am nervous about stumbling. If I blunder, defeat falls solely on my slumped shoulders. And I have never preferred to blame myself for being a loser. However, when God is the frontline banner, he is also the God who tops the treacherous hills first, welcoming the most formidable blows, so we remain whole.

The first soldiers up and over the hills in battle face a higher chance of injury and death. The enemy is fully intact, steady, and ready. If you dive back into U.S. history, D-Day is an undeniable example of the sheer bravery and heroism a soldier must embody to invade the enemy in the wide-open territory. France's beaches were calm as the U.S. soldiers approached the shore by boat, but the moment they made advancements toward the sand, the Germans had their guns, tanks, and firebombs ready.

The U.S. soldiers were fully exposed to German threats, yet they knew all along their mission was to advance through the fire and take Germany's base. The Omaha Wave, the United States' first wave of soldiers to enter this deathly battleground, took the most brutal hit. Following the war, the Omaha Wave was coined the "suicide wave." Hundreds of soldiers died at a clip, but one soldier's heroism strongly grips me even amid this terror.

First Lieutenant Jimmie W. Monteith Jr. of the 16th Infantry, 1st Infantry Division didn't hold a high rank, and as far as GI Joe appearances go, he wasn't the most dashing man in uniform. He fit neither status nor stature of what most would consider a superior fighter. Yet, his bravery as they stormed Normandy's beaches resulted in one of the highest military honors a soldier received following the Normandy Invasion.

Monteith Jr. wasn't honored for charging straight toward the enemy but for running a horizontal pattern, side to side, on the beach, cheering his men on, encouraging them to continue into the mouth of hell despite the hellfire raining down on them. He championed the men up and over their first hurdle, but Monteith Jr. didn't stop there.

Allied Forces couldn't bring the same amount of weaponry to this fight as they knew the Germans would have. The Allies arrived by boat, so, needless to say, the U.S. didn't haul the same firepower as the Germans. Each big-boy weapon was a prize that must be protected and used with great accuracy. Monteith Jr. spotted two tanks under heavy fire by German enemies. Bullets and bombs scattered all around these tanks, leaving soldiers frozen, defenseless, unable to move forward. Yet, Monteith Jr. ran straight into this madness and, by foot, urged the tanks on. He willingly led the drivers through a known German minefield—and to his success, these men passed another hurdle. The men under Monteith Jr.'s leadership gained an advantageous position that day, and eventually, the Allies claimed one of the most heroic wins of all U.S. military history.

Though thousands of Allied forces died at the Battle of Normandy, they stole the victory. Thus, the tide of the war turned in favor of freedom.

My soul feels that Monteith Jr. is a near-spitting image of our God on the battlefield. Yes, God goes first, taking the brunt of hell's worst. Still, I also believe he runs a horizontal pattern, encouraging us to keep going, keep fighting, keep moving forward, and remember that victory in the name of freedom is a glory that never dies. And it's a glory we share with and for others. Victory in the name of liberty is the gospel. Meanwhile, God calls us to be Monteith Jr.'s, too, not because we are the pivoting factors of the war, but because Christianity has never hinged on anything but selflessness, sacrifice, and love.

Our win with God might not measure up to earthly standards, but it will remain eternally glorious—and soldiers like Monteith Jr. discovered that such glory was the pinnacle of fulfillment. No need for control and no need to fear when God leads the charge. The gospel never asks us to control the situation; it simply compels us to act, fight for love, and show up when we can't guarantee we won't walk away wounded. Monteith Jr. knew, no doubt, that death was a high probability, but freedom meant more. Even at the mouth of hell itself, Monteith Jr. saw a piece of heaven, an end goal that led to life, and he knew his sacrifice was worth such a prize.

Much like the Israelites in Exodus, we aren't the best soldiers, but we are free from the law because we fight for love. Heavenly strength rests in the decision to fight our battles God's way, allowing truth, honor, and love to lead. We no longer need our itinerary, budget, or game plan. Just as Normandy's chaos crushed any fine-tuned, laid-out plans for Monteith Jr., he still knew to act. He wasn't so tied to the original strategy that he negated what must be done despite the chaos. Instead, he let love, honor, and sacrifice pave the plan.

You must know how Monteith Jr. fared on D-Day once he navigated the tanks through Germany's minefield. The words below are a snippet of the official military statement drafted to honor Monteith Jr. for his bravery:

> *He then rejoined his company, and under his leadership, his men captured an advantageous position on the hill. Supervising the defense of his newly won position against repeated vicious counter-attacks, he continued to ignore his own personal safety, repeatedly crossing the 200 or 300 yards of open terrain under heavy fire to strengthen links in his defensive chain. When the enemy succeeded in completely surrounding 1st Lt. Monteith and his unit and while leading the fight out of the situation, 1st Lt. Monteith was killed by enemy fire. The courage, gallantry, and intrepid leadership displayed by 1st Lt. Monteith is worthy of emulation.*[1]

We are free to fight without the weight of ourselves holding us back. We can choose to emulate Monteith Jr.'s courage when we are equipped with God's invincible weaponry, when we get behind the Banner and say with complete confidence, "God, I'm right behind you."

Everyday Application:

1. How do you define Jehovah Nissi? What does it mean that "the Lord is [your] Banner"?

2. Considering the three detrimental prerequisites that Christ's love dissolves—the need to have all the answers, the need to fear, the need to fight for the law—which one still cripples you most? How can God, as Jehovah Nissi, dismantle that unnecessary prerequisite in your life?

3. Though none of us can ever be a WWII soldier who stormed Normandy's shores, how can we be brave in the places and spaces we navigate, like Monteith Jr.?

4. "... because we fight for love we are free from the law." How can being free to accept grace despite flaws free you in your daily life?

---

1. "History: The United States Army," sect. "D-Day," para. 6

Prayer Closet Thought:

Make a list of the two people you allow to occupy most of your time. If possible, list two people you don't live with, two who aren't family. Once you've listed your two people, consider if they would be willing to hold up your arms in the fight. Do they always take but never give? Or are they loyal and ready to stick by your side when times are tough? Often, friendships can aid in making or breaking pivotal parts of your faith. As Psalm 1 suggests, keep wise company. And if your friends don't reflect such support and encouragement, it's time to pursue healthier relationships.

13

Little, Tiny Miracles

※

"I COULD USE A LITTLE miracle today."

"We're so grateful for this tiny miracle."

"I'm thankful for the small miracle in a sunrise."

Humans love the idea of bite-sized glory. Perhaps we want a miracle small enough for us to see, hold, and carry in our backpacks for the hard days. After all, we have a tough time walking in faith—we prefer the sight of God's goodness, a spiritual yet tangible affirmation that Truth is good and worth stepping into each day. I believe we shrink miracles in our effort at quietly dodging the possibility of "big" miracles, while resting assured in the "small" ones. In other words, we want a safe, predictable faith, one that fits snug inside the rhythm and reason of human explanation.

Jesus called his disciples to witness miracles, even perform them in his name through the power of the Holy Spirit, yet we hope God limits our calling to the mundane. We want blessings available for convenience's sake, but when miracles require our faithful efforts, we retreat to routine rhythms. Why so shallow and fearful? What would miracles be apart from our ability to embrace the unexpected, uncomfortable, and impossible?

There's a humbling, somewhat frightening notion that if we allow all miracles to be big miracles, inviting them to invade our schedules, hopes, and dreams, we must face that our world runs off a power grid outside our control. Far beyond the Milky Way, our fate lies in the hands of an Almighty God who knows the name of each star from the cosmos. Suppose we embrace such a holy, rather irrational definition. In that case, this is no longer a god limited to answering huffy prayers about mountains of bills and minuscule measures of hope as we deal with the in-laws.

No, this is now the God who moves chains of mountains by his mere thought; this is the God who never provides anything less than a cup that runs over. And if this humbling, terrifying, and rather alluring fantasy is truth, we must accept faith in Christ with the same bullet-proof anticipation as a wide-eyed child who believes in Kris Kringle. We must deny our limited vision, our controlled space, just as youthful innocence denies sleep and thwarts the naysaying classmates to hold out for Santa's late-night visit.

Nature herself practices the art of welcoming faithful miracles, calling them big, bold, and life-changing, even if they recur each day:

Something inside the farmhouse rooster knows the brimming, beaming golden light that silently swaddles the grass in all its glory is a faithful but big miracle. Its wonders compel him to sing a rather squawky song, beckoning the whole world to wake up before missing this daily majesty.

The oceans, the waters that engulf three-fourths of our planet, draw us in each night, following the command of the moon to reach the sand's surface, begging us to gather around and see what beauty she spits back on dry ground. The oceans do not feel threatened by the moon; instead, they feel they have a calling from the Creator to fulfill the miracle of bringing treasures to shore day in, day out.

The Big Dipper knows full well her spot will never change. She is planted on a specific grid of the galaxies until the end of time, and yet, she shows up each night to beam a bright, beautiful wonder. Though her view never changes, she allows her perspective to grow, compelling the world to praise a limitless God. She remains a daily dependable that reminds us just how small yet significant we are in the eyes of our tender Maker.

Do we have a healthy habit of noticing these wonders? Or are they simply the "things" that happen as we go about our more important daily tasks? Who needs shooting stars when we have a dishwasher to unload? Why notice the sunrise when your phone calls for its blue light attention? Why gather seashells when there are social media followers to collect? Many of us are waiting on miracles that fit our agenda, our profile for hope. Yet, hope glistens all around us. Confirmation of God's goodness is above us, behind us, beside us. It's everywhere. Unfortunately, it often takes facing something drastic, somewhat dangerous, and downright scary for us to stop our daily tasks long enough to think, "That might've been a miracle. A *big* one."

It seems the Israelites lost their touch with miracles too. Sure, they had witnessed the Red Sea bust open, allowing them to cross the sea's floor completely dry. They saw Pharoah's army engulfed by the same waters they safely evaded. Israel knew miracles, the kind we deem "big." But they had their roadmap, their bridled version of spiritual benefits—and the next token they would consider big and booming lived on the other side of the desert, safe and sound within the bounds of the Promised Land. They negated bread that fell from the sky each day, the flock of quail swooping in from seemingly nowhere to offer protein, lasting sustenance as they wandered in the wilderness. And the cloud of God's presence in the day and his Spirit's bursting light to guide them at night—nah, that happened every day. That was a "small," expected, practically mandated miracle.

In the name of expectation, we negate the love behind miracles. When we assume we deserve them, we throw them in our backpacks and move along with our plans. They are the small, measurable, dependable ones because they show up each day. Why should we consider the love and sacrifice behind them? Surely, ground-breaking effort can't be thrown into something reproduced daily, right?

Wrong. Heartbreakingly wrong. This damaged perception of mandatory yet mundane miracles thrives off a contaminated petri dish where humanity grows a detrimental concoction of false gratitude. When we expect goodness, we degrade its purpose. Instead of allowing grace and beauty and wonder to embody us every day, we have treated the kindness and love necessary for these things to grow as nobility. In other words, praise be those who are kind—as if it's some rare feat only the religious ones dare enact. Meanwhile, praise be me because I'm worthy of the lovely ones showering me with selflessness. I deserve the miracles, but don't ask if I willingly play a part in someone else's.

Often, as we are begging for miracles, they show up in those around us. Other times, others are begging for miracles, but they only show up the second we answer God's call to love well. How often do we pray to be part of the miracle rather than beg for our own?

Most days, it's a take-but-no-give relationship we offer to God's miracles, and yet, we mandate a give-but-no-take relationship from others. May I let you in on a secret? Kindness has never been nobility; instead, it has always been a necessity, a holy mandate, to offer the world a fireproof antidote for its weary, grumbling soul. Kindness is the miracle—the big one. The one we see in nature that provides us with glory each day, no matter how routine it is for her. The one we see in a God who gives of himself to humans who fare so poorly in the spiritual realm that even rocks and trees sing his praises before we do. And yet, he sent his Son to die a brutal death for a near-silent, lackadaisical people.

We have not only forgotten but have actively chosen to limit miracles. To call them small. To show up small. To say they are just enough to give us what we need without daring us to step out of our comforts. Yet, there are times when God grows weary in waiting for us to step forward, to step out in immense faith. Can you blame him? Sometimes, he nudges us on with big miracles, begging us to call them what they are: indescribable, unimaginable, only God-orchestrated. Yet many times, the only miracles we slow down to identify are those wonderstruck moments that shake our day and follow scary, fearful experiences:

As newbies to Colorado—from mid-west Georgia's muggy steam— Josh and I took great caution while driving in snow, particularly ice. Coming from a state that shuts down the world when tiny flurries fall from the sky, never sticking to the ground, we can't call ourselves pros at navigating tundra-like elements. But what's strange about Colorado is just how unpredictable its weather can be. You see, living in the valley of the Rockies, your day's climate hinges on which way the wind rolls off the mountains. If the high altitude creates a wonky pressure as the wind from the mountaintops presses down, you could get anything from a hail storm to a blizzard. Meanwhile, just seconds before this cold chaos, it's normal to stroll around in sunny, sixty-five-degree weather. Climate changes here are rapid and unpredictable, and you can't always prepare for the instant stress they ensue.

By God's grace, our first winter in Colorado was what the locals called "strange" and "mild." We didn't experience an actual snow day until late January. The clouds were heavy and gray, not like rain clouds, though. They carried a puffy, thick haze, suspending anticipation over our small town of Fountain. Then, not too far into the day, tiny snowflakes fluttered from the sky as I walked the pups. The flakes gained speed, collecting in powdered piles on the grass, rocks, and streets. It was a beautiful sight, a rare one in Georgia. My only fear in this wanderlust scene was Josh not returning from work in one piece. Shortly after my stroll with Alfie and Daisy, I received a call that he was headed my way. The snow didn't seem treacherous, so he had time to make it back before snow fogged his route home.

Not fifteen minutes after his first call, I received another call that he had been in a wreck. Thankfully, he was fully intact, though I can't say the same for our little white adventure car, Cloud. Due to the snow, several large vehicles in front of Josh lost traction, fish-tailing and flailing all over the interstate. The largest vehicle in front of Josh was a semi-truck. The truck's body swung a horizontal pattern, blocking both lanes of the interstate, leaving Josh and three other vehicles at the mercy of dodging into the banks.

Yet, my Josh didn't dive off the side of the road. He would have plowed into the people stuck in the other damaged vehicles if he had done that. Instead, Josh thought it was best to stay the course. As a result, he ran straight into the semi's bed so he wouldn't risk hurting anyone. The passenger side of our vehicle took the most consequential blow; airbags deployed, and the windshield completely caved. Yet, Josh's driver's side remained untouched. He walked away from a picture of death with bruises, scratches, and a sore arm and ribcage, but nothing fatal.

I had been on the phone, frantically explaining to family and close friends the treacherous events of the day. While describing the perfect angle Cloud hit the semi to avoid being clipped by the massive front-end of the truck, I went to call it a "small" miracle. But I couldn't finish the sentence. Calling this a "small" miracle felt like a low blow toward God, like an Olympian showing off a gold medal and having his own mother say, "That's a lot smaller than I imagined it would be."

This quiet revelation echoed in my brain over the next several days as people consistently checked on Josh. Thanks to the tender concern of others, I was able to practice embracing all miracles as big miracles over and over:

"Yes, it was nothing other than a miracle that I wasn't in the car with him, taking the big blow on the passenger side. I'm not sure I would've made it if I had been in the car with him."

"Yes, it was definitely a miracle that the driver's side of the car was left untouched."

"Josh, do you realize that was a miracle?"

Miracles are miracles; I now remind myself. There's no need for "small," "tiny," "little," "baby"—none of that. God's ability and delight in defying the impossible are never meager or measurable by our measly standards.

With such in mind, I say:

Life is a series of miracles that we might define as mundane, even expected, but that doesn't make them miniscule. For perspective, let's delve into the first habitual miracle you experience each day: opening your eyes.

The Creation Studies Institute shares that "The actual anatomy of sight is a wonderful example of what Intelligent Design theorists and Creationists call 'irreducible complexity.' The optic nerve is attached to the sclera or white of the eye. The optic nerve is also known as cranial nerve II and is a continuation of the axons of the ganglion cells in the retina. There are approximately 1.1 million nerve cells in each optic nerve. The optic nerve, which acts like a cable connecting the eyes with the brain, actually is more like brain tissue than it is nerve tissue."[1]

In layman's terms, before you've snagged that morning cup of brew, millions of nerve cells have already activated, allowing you to spot the sunrise and fumble through the closet to find your work clothes.

I'm not so sure each day is a series of tiny miracles. I believe each day is a miraculous orchestration of stringed events directed by the Composer of all irrationally beautiful things.

Perspective is key to appreciating miracles, yet miracles aren't defined by my ability to process them. They aren't so small that I must stop to notice them. They need no magnifying glass, no microscope. Rather, they are so big that I must stop to absorb their magnitude.

For instance, though mommas and daddies are blown away by their "tiny" miracle child, this human is a full-blown miracle. Mommas, without humankind's control, a microscopic sperm met your egg, and a human developed all necessary body parts while being attached to an internal chord you didn't provide on your own. When you sucked in oxygen, the baby sucked in oxygen. When you ate, the baby ate. When you laughed, your joy echoed in its developing brain over and over until it realized you were Mom. And the moment that tiny creature breathed oxygen on its own, it didn't need an introduction from you. A one-day-old human with no experience in communication magically knew the only human it wanted to lull it to sleep was you. That's a big, magical miracle, mommas.

I sometimes wonder if our hard days wouldn't feel so heavy if we permitted miracles to be significant. If we embraced the reality that our finite standards don't control our God. Maybe that doesn't mean we get the miracle we specifically asked for, or the one needed to fulfill x, y, or z. Still, the biggest blessing of all big miracles is knowing that we are never absent from the impossible becoming possible. We are forever loved and guarded by the powerful Creator who isn't subject to small blessings, hindered by our failures, or intimidated and slowed down by roadblocks. Our Creator is

1. Creation Studies Institute, sect. "Complex System of the Eye," para. 4

good, kind, faithful, honest, just, loving, and selfless, and each miracle that follows his command is subject to his powerful nature.

There is a rare goodness behind the wildflower that blooms despite the chill. There is kind energy behind your eyes prodding you to start the day. There's a transcendent faithfulness in a big ball of light, this burning center of our solar system, that has yet to be late to work and always leaves right on time. There is a gentle honesty in a body that rejects unhealthy foods we try to force down. There remains a just purpose behind why someone has a wreck texting and driving yet survives. There is a loving reason we are granted a heart that doesn't need our help to beat. There's also selflessness to the air that lends us oxygen in forceless hopes that we will return the favor with carbon dioxide.

Maybe the biggest question, my most gnawing thought, is what would happen if we were humbled by simply waking up each morning? What if we trusted in a good God and asked him for the impossible—not the reasonable, but the impossible? Maybe, in those moments of somewhat awkward, likely doubtful prayers, we opened our eyes to discover miracles have never left us, have never parted from us. What if we saw God and his everlasting presence as the motherboard miracle?

With God and his unmatched authority guiding our hearts, shaping our lives to fit a glorious design, I challenge us all to embrace God's miracles we fear most. Yes, the biggest miracles. Then, and only then, does our faith become sight, a tangible marvel confirming God's loving rule over the impossible.

Everyday Application:

1. Do you, like me, find yourself labeling miracles as small or tiny? If so, which ones tend to get this label and why?

2. Which moment in your life has been the "big" miracle moment? Did it change the way you see both big and small miracles? Or was it easy to fall back into ignoring the reoccurring miracles we experience?

3. Are you ever like the morning rooster, announcing to everyone that it's time to stop and notice the miracles of life regardless of how you sound? If not, how can you start welcoming these miracles into your routine?

4. Are you willing to grant miracles the permanent permission to always and forever be big?

Prayer Closet Thought:

This is a simple, one-day challenge. All you need is paper and pen. For one day, and one day only, keep track of all the things in your life that wouldn't be possible without God. Every chance you get (not while driving, of course), jot down the things outside mankind's control that make the world tick. At the end of the day, revisit that list. Thank God for each of those things. And remember, every single item on that list is a big ole miracle.

14

A Watchtower

※

I DARESAY THE ISRAELITES were a presumptuous people. If their academic studies included anything resembling modern cotillion delicacies, it is plenty safe to say they failed each lesson in etiquette. They were brassy in their demand for forgiveness, with repentance rarely making a genuine debut among these rebellious masses. They demanded God's presence, but doubted his goodness and begged for his deliverance, never mastering a heart of thanksgiving. As often as I roll my eyes at their mediocre faith, I must accept that I see their story from a 20,000-foot view, both hindsight and the post-resurrection climate aiding my judgmental perception.

The desert floor can shield no secret from the mountaintop, summit forever holding optic advantage over sand. Nature, history, and nearly everything point to such pinnacles. The higher you climb, the keener the view. The higher the altitude, the safer you are. You can see all there is at a perfect 360-degree angle, but few predators, creeping, crawling creatures, and the like, can survive so far above the earth's less extreme elevation.

Where I live, in Fountain, Colorado, the altitude rests around 5,500 feet. This vertical separation from sea level is high enough that fleas cannot survive. The pressure of thinning air causes their itty-bitty bodies to explode, quite literally. Thus, this climate provides maximum safety for my pups year-round. Higher altitude also limits the variety (or lack thereof) of plants and flowers that can thrive in the rocky soil. Colorado doesn't host lush, green-stemmed petals of purple and pink; it houses thinned, bristle-like bushes that allow you to see anything and everything right under your feet. This not-so botanical terrain offers a life-saving vantage since snakes are more prevalent in the desert-like landscape of southern Colorado.

Though heights make my stomach lurch, even I have difficulty denying the upper hand tall spaces provide. Aside from my fear of losing my grounding and falling to a grotesque death, I must admit that heights seem to separate me from myself. Such humility is rare yet beautiful, shrinking life's worries and stretching its wonder. Not that I have an out-of-body experience, but humility has more room to thrive when the span of a great, wide world envelops my microscopic being.

In the past, if you asked me to toss around a few microscopic characters in the Bible, I would throw Habakkuk's name in the hat, or perhaps not. Most of us forget Habakkuk exists, such a little book featuring a minor prophet, with little recognition behind the pulpit. If you were to ask any solid theological question regarding Habakkuk's text, all I could say is I know scholars, and not-so scholarly folks, argue about the last "k" of the book's name. They host heated conversations on whether or not the caboose consonant is pronounced or left silent. Until recently, I knew no life-changing wisdom, no wondrous perception of the truths hiding in Habakkuk's three small chapters.

I discovered a three-week study of Habakkuk written by The Daily Grace Co.'s Kristin Schmucker, *Even If*, and less than one week into the curriculum, I felt shame. Shame for assuming small things, minor prophets, small spaces, can't hold groundbreaking change, the type of change that doesn't simply bind wounds but heals them too.

Habakkuk is one of the first and only biblical characters to supply the near-perfect echo of today's one big question, the one brutal, heartbroken thought that crosses every human's mind: why does a good God allow bad things to happen? Those who accept and reject the Christian faith wrestle with this nagging thought. I believe this is the make-or-break point in one's decision to follow Christ. A person answers this question with an honest reply that they aren't sure, yet they choose to believe in God's sovereign goodness. Meanwhile, others who face this question and can't find the black-and-white answer cling to a disheartening solution: God remains distant from humanity's suffering. Thus, he isn't as loving as others claim.

This question, or perhaps its mysterious answer, reserves a spot in each person's soul as a consistent, unavoidable wrestling that undeniably emerges due to humans feeling the diabolical weight of a fallen world. Such a place daily reminds man of the aches and pains of sin and selfishness, a place that inflicts the sickness of body and soul on the just and unjust.

However, before plunging into the spiritual weight of this book, a small history lesson is necessary: historians believe Habakkuk likely prophesied to the children of Israel during the first five years of King Jehoiakim's reign, around the time of 609 BC. Jehoiakim was a ruthless, evil king, a man who manipulated his status and dodged any notion that his people were called to honor their God, the God who had brought them out of Egypt and into the Promised Land. Less than two centuries prior, the northern kingdom of Jerusalem had fallen, and Judah remained on shaky ground.

An evil, ruthless king, a dilapidated kingdom, little sign of any hope, and what does God ask Habakkuk to prophesy to his people? The Babylonians were going to invade soon. (Not to spoil the timeline, but Habakkuk's prophecy came true close to the end of his five-year calling. In 605 BC, the Babylonians invaded, causing a destructive blow to Israel. But that was only a minor battle. The Babylonians came back roughly twenty-five years later to cause total devastation.)

Though this book's historical setting hosts the very essence of doom and gloom, what I love about Habakkuk is that these three chapters are a back-and-forth dialogue between the minor prophet and God. It's solely a conversation, but it's raw and vulnerable. It doesn't offer proverbial antidotes, doesn't hold any accounts of vast, New Testament-style miracles. These three chapters are simply a lament of man's limits and a desperate hope that God is better than we could imagine.

Habakkuk asks the one bold question most of us fear to process, and God provides an answer. The answer. Now, some of you might feel a twinge of jealousy, myself included, from time to time, as we think: God hasn't answered my question yet. I'm choosing to believe in his goodness, but why can't he provide the insight, the application to offer a more tangible hope? Why did God share wisdom with Habakkuk, yet he remains silent when I need to know why he permits my pain and suffering?

I would be amiss, cold, and heartless if I didn't confess that I have these unsettling, rather frustrating conversations with God each time my life isn't "flutter ponds and lily trees" as my great-grandfather, Oliver, would say. However, when I want to chase this rabbit hole of bitterness, assuming God is distant, two of my countering thoughts materialize from the crannies of hope my heart crawls to on hard days. These countering thoughts, these itty-bitty bits of light, I feel led to share with you:

A lack of answers is an abundance of pursuit. I've heard that God doesn't mind the complex, personal questions we hurl his way. God welcomes such wild intensity. Why? Because you only ask questions if you want the answers. This is an elementary truth we see displayed throughout the entire world of academia. The students who want good grades pursue the solutions. They are the ones who will try and retry a math equation until they understand the answer. They are the ones who will stop by the professor's office if they are stumped. On the other hand, those who don't care about their GPA scrape by with the knowledge they already have, a need for answers not quite a need, nonetheless a want.

Such truth spills over into romantic relationships as well. When a man is not interested in a woman yet wants to remain polite and gentlemanly, he offers a simple "How are you?". When the woman provides a reply, he smiles and carries on with his day, gallant yet satisfied with nothing more from her answer. If something about a woman's presence catches his attention, his questions won't stop with a basic, somewhat required "How are you?". Instead, he will ask about her coffee choice, ask if he can grab a napkin after her French vanilla dark roast spills all over the barista's counter, and ask if he can hold the door for her on her way out of the cafe. If she seems openly responsive to his kindness, he will ask if he can get her phone number and take her to dinner. From there, more profound, more vulnerable questions ensue. Answers surface. A relationship forms. A relationship grows. A relationship becomes so priceless that it takes vows before God to remain steadfast and noble until the end.

Pursuit parallels purpose. What we crave, what we desire, where we find our purpose is wrapped in what we chase. Though a lack of answers feels unsatisfying, a great pursuit of God's character reflects a tainted yet passionate heart that cares to know the Maker better.

Though God sums up our ignorance in Isaiah 55:8–9, "'For my thoughts are not your thoughts, neither are your ways my ways,' declares the Lord. 'As the heavens are higher than the earth, so are my ways higher than your ways and my thoughts than your thoughts,'" I imagine his perfect paternal nature chuckles when we counter this truth with, "But why?".

Such was Habakkuk's childlike pursuit. Even though he was a prophet appointed by God to share his hope, he knew Judah was threatened by the vicious Chaldeans (also known as the Babylonians in other books). With their violent, ruthless nature threatening Israel's promise for freedom, Habakkuk remained human enough to inquire: "God, but are you sure we are safe? Why do you let the Chaldeans bully us? Why do you allow bad people to hurt good people—*Your* people? Why does a good God let bad things happen?".

The answer is held in the eyes of the One you are questioning—in the heart of Yahweh.

Perhaps the ignorance of praying from the ground floor stirred Habakkuk to discover a mountaintop view, where perspective was keener, and the enemy had no hopes of a sneak attack. After Habakkuk asked God why he allows bad things to happen, Habakkuk 2:1–2 recorded the prophet's words of waiting: "I will stand at my watch and station myself on the ramparts; I will look to see what he will say to me, and what answer I am to give to this complaint."

A rampart is a giant, defensive wall offering thick protection to a castle, town, or village from various enemy weapons. Habakkuk climbed to the watchtower of this rocky fortress to stand guard against the Chaldeans and find a fresh perspective and a more humble place to ask God a blunt, desperate question. He, too, understood that the mountaintop provides a more accurate perception, a safer place for answers.

Scholars admit they aren't sure just how long Habakkuk waited in his watchtower for God's response, but they are positive this is where he received God's holy reply. Regardless, acquiring this answer from God while waiting in the tower required much of Habakkuk, demanding both action and leadership.

While God never prioritizes works over faith, and salvation is through faith in Christ alone, we are called to prepare our hearts to hear from God. An abundant pursuit of who he is takes striving efforts and active patience. It sounds strange, the act of waiting to embody a powerful verb with spiritual legs. Yet, preparing your heart to wait for God's reply is the most powerful communication tool between heaven and earth that we have as humans. Moreover, this righteous pursuit of patience creates an inviting atmosphere, a peace amid the storm, drawing outsiders into love. It's a double-edged yet righteous sword, piercing lies and driving truth to its hilt for God's children to champion. Pursuing God, waiting on his goodness, is spiritual leadership and victory, especially in the face of life's most burdensome questions.

Habakkuk confirms this truth in chapter 2, verse 3, when he says, "For the revelation awaits an appointed time; it speaks of the end and will not prove false. Though it linger, wait for it; it will certainly come and will not delay."

Again, though scholars confess they cannot offer a concrete timeline for Habakkuk's waiting, I believe he climbed up and down the watchtower each day, begging and praying this would be the day he received his answer. This is the sort of spiritual desperation, this hunger for God that never leaves us empty. Habakkuk chose to believe God was not delayed, not distant but preparing a life-altering time for him to receive the answer.

We aren't subjected to climbing up and down a rampart like Habakkuk, but when we climb up and down our mountain, day after day, actively pining after God's answer, this is a faith in motion. This is our sealed salvation in action. Clinging to a God we don't fully understand but choose to recklessly pursue because of his undeniable, unshakeable love for mankind.

Faith, in its raw, valid form, is messy. It's a roll-up-your-sleeves sort of noun that demands you conjugate its verb, settling for nothing less than a permanent active tense. This is why James says that faith without works is dead. James 2:14–17 pens these infamous verses:

"What good is it, my brothers and sisters, if someone claims to have faith but has no deeds? Can such faith save them? Suppose a brother or a sister is without clothes and daily food. If one of you says to them, 'Go in peace; keep warm and well fed,' but does nothing about their physical needs, what good is it? In the same way, faith by itself, if it is not accompanied by action, is dead."

James wasn't weighing merit above God's mercy as a means of true salvation, but after walking with Christ, he was sure that truly loving him, believing him to be the Son of God, would ignite a glorious revolution. This cataclysmic collide of heaven kissing earth with impossibility defied the finite. Life defeated death and rolled the onerous stone away. Such a faith would spark a spiritual flame that we would stoke, that we would throw the wood on, over and over again, if only to feel the gentle warmth and hear a whisper from his Holy Spirit.

His voice would be our vice, and such a vice would be so lovely we would volunteer to weather winter's brutal cold to chop the firewood. Such loveliness wouldn't always answer our questions but would aid our wanderings through the wilderness. And such an aid, once our strivings and wanderings cease on this earth, would lead us home, to a place where we have the answers and have him, our omniscient Creator and Sustainer, the Almighty God.

The most revered name for God in Jewish culture was, and remains, Yahweh. This word is so powerful that Jews will not speak the name aloud.

One dare not let such a holy name leave unholy lips, and justly so. Millennia later, this reverence holds strong in Jewish custom. And though I do not claim Judaism as my religion, I am in awe of their majestical view of God. He is so righteous, holy, and pure that perhaps some of his names better remain unsaid on this side of heaven.

This beautiful picture of God, the High Priest, simultaneously calls me to worship him as my dearest friend. Despite my understanding and love of this Jewish custom regarding Yahweh, I find him to be the Friend who dotes on any endearment I offer. Meanwhile, such a loyal Companion abides with me when I don't reciprocate such loyalty when sin's most cunning lies mask my best efforts at love. This Companion also remains by my side when I have asked every question and yelled every bitter thought his way. He still loves me enough to provide answers that extend security amid this world's consuming chaos.

Though I have stressed faith's crucial element of patience, undoubtedly, you are ready for God's answer to Habakkuk. One of the most enchanting, near-magical parts of Habakkuk is a resolve we can apply to our realities. This big, booming question that has weathered the world's worst and still craves to make sense of it can be answered in a tiny verse nestled in Habakkuk 2:4. It's a verse I have complete faith you have heard ten times over: "See, the enemy is puffed up; his desires are not upright—but the righteous person will live by his faithfulness."

Often, we believe "the righteous will live by faith" is an epiphany reserved for Paul in Romans 1:17, but here, the reader recognizes faith as the answer to our why. The "why" can only be found in who. And until we pursue the who, until we have faith in who will answer, his answer will never be enough to ease our hearts.

In essence, God replies to Habakkuk, "Hold tight. I know what I'm doing. Remember, I am the God of goodness and grace. I have a desperate adoration for you and My people. Allow me to be God. Wait."

The more I understand God's goodness, the more I choose goodness in my own life. If we, as an international body of believers, the whole Church, would allow God's goodness to permeate our daily actions, the tide could turn, and people would feel less inclined to ask why so many bad things happen. What if holy strivings caused our perception of tragedies to cease? What if love outlived hate? Hope would lead the way, lingering at the forefront of our thoughts, propelling a righteous reason for our actions.

Why do bad things happen? What I find more pivotal is contemplating why good things don't happen. If we have free will, what are we not curating to create a sustainable peace with one another? Despite the bad, goodness would show up, its presence bolder, its impact eternal, if our solutions weren't winning digital debates and offering a helping hand to the enemy.

I believe you can find hope and the resolution to life's strivings in the last three verses in the book of Habakkuk. In Habakkuk 3:17–19, he proclaims, "Though the fig tree does not bud and there are no grapes on the vines, though the olive crop fails and the fields produce no food, though are no sheep in the pen and no cattle in the stalls, yet I will rejoice in the Lord, I will be joyful in God my Savior. The Sovereign Lord is my strength; he makes my feet like the feet of a deer, he enables me to tread on the heights."

Whether Habakkuk's people had food or not, whether they had animals for religious sacrifices or not, God's strength, who he was (and is), was the only answer Habakkuk needed in the end. There wasn't, "Wait, God. What about the first part? You didn't answer my original question."

No, because in the end, the hunger, thirst, and mediocre faith of Habakkuk created a parched yet perfect avenue for God's omniscience to restore all that was lost, both on earth and in heaven. Exhaustion and Exile met God in Habakkuk's watchtower. Sure, the heights concealed the answers for a while, forcing Habakkuk to climb back down to the dusty earth floor each night, but when Exhaustion and Exile met the God of the galaxies, he replied: "My children tread on the heights" (Hab 3:19).

Exile and Exhaustion paused, the ferocious fraternal twins unsure what to say. To their shock, God never planned to banish their existence, but he instilled a purpose of growth within their lifelessness. Before their minds riddled a rival response, God's kindness replied, "Let's make beauty from your ashes" (Isa 61:3).

God's majestic kindness locks eyes with Exile and Exhaustion as he further delves: "The wilderness' sole purpose was to beckon my children to the mountaintop, to give them a reason to tread steep ground for glory, to trade lifeless, even-paved ground, for the wondrous adventure of the unknown. You, Exhaustion and Exile, aren't the villains. You're the catalysts for empathy, vulnerability, and change. Do you not recall that empathy drew my Son to earth? Vulnerability made him both God and man. Change was offered to the world the moment he defeated sin, Satan, and death. I beckon you, yes, even you, Exile and Exhaustion, to be malleable. Fall apart in My hands. Let me perform a new work through you. Own your unknown, a place well-known, strategically cultivated, rich with purpose, created by Me—the Author of all good stories, beginning, middle, and healed ever after."

Everyday Application:

1. What does it mean that "a lack of answers is an abundance of pursuit"?

2. When we actively choose to see God's goodness each day, goodness naturally exudes from us. Which areas of your life have negativity and gloom invaded? Could it be that frustration and a bad attitude, on your part, is why you feel as though bad things always happen to good people?

3. Once you identify your doom-and-gloom areas, create hands-on ways to doubt the doubts and embrace hope.

4. Reading Habakkuk 3:19, "My children tread on the heights," what are some impossible places you never thought you could reach but not for God? What impossible areas have you still not reached?

Prayer Closet Thought:

I've never truly experienced a flawless season that wasn't stricken with some result of a fallen world: financial struggles, car wrecks, scary medical appointments, terrible dogs, career frustrations, etc. I'm reasonably confident your life has been the same way. With reality and the ever-present enemy to our hearts and souls, what are you facing now that has you so desperate for healing that you would climb an actual tower to talk to God? Day in and day out, you would climb up and down the ladder, convinced this is your only hope for healing.

Good news—God is a hope that never wavers, and you don't need a tower similar to Habakkuk's to hear from God. Remember the prayer closet we discussed in chapter 1? That is your tower. God is your hope. Visit that prayer closet day in and day out and allow your raw, honest conversations with God to be willed with confidence in his hope.

15

The Path Home

※

I WISH I WERE as kind to non-fiction writing as I am to my historical fiction novels. I enter the realm of a World War II refugee woman whose kindness melts the heart of a runaway Russian soldier, culture curating no hatred between the two. I embrace all gothic drama encapsulating the life of the Brooklyn Bridge lead engineer's wife, daring to believe the nonsensical drama that she had a near-fling with Mr. Barnum, the circus man. I gawk when no one has time for a love triangle between a 1940s nurse and two dashing U.S. servicemen vying for her affection. I show up to this fantastical ink-and-page land fully prepared to be struck by love and whisked through a world of strivings resolved.

Though these characters are tucked behind walls of fantasy and impossibility, they also showcase devastating qualities and survive the most gruesome scenes. Hope amid the gloom, an authentic look into the human's raw, genuine soul, is what draws me into their stories. It's not the magic of time travel or manipulation of history that rivets my reader's heart. Nor is it romance that leaves a permanent mark in my mind. Rather, their survival holds me captive for hundreds and hundreds of pages, crushing my soul when resolve forces me to leave their world tucked between the book's covers.

Survival reminds us the most tragic accounts can't negate goodness. After all, survival means life faces death and still wins another sunrise. These characters survive life's lowest blows with hearts that still beat and feel and believe that the next breath is worth taking because it might welcome a miracle. After terrible decisions or uncontrollable chaos, such endurance beckons me to understand more of who they are—and how I can mirror such stamina on my journey with Christ.

But I can't say I treat non-fiction, particularly Christian literature, with the same wide-eyed grace. Though this is my writer's realm, where I find purpose and thrive in what I unwillingly call my talent, this isn't a space where I always feel community. I feel God's presence as I share his heart, beating out gentle messages across my laptop's black-and-white keys. Regardless, this is my niche because it's my calling, not because it has created an inclusive, non-stereotypical body of people I easily trust with theology and grace-filled truth. I am cautious of whose "Jesus words" take root inside my heart.

However, I can't fight the urge to peruse each bookstore's Christian Living section. Most often, a colorful yet thinner spine catches my eye. A piece of me hesitates to pluck the twinkling title from its place, but my conscience says this could be a creative way to get out of the Bible study funk when I want to further understand God without plowing through heavy chunks of Scripture.

Conscience wins out, and I slowly flip to the book's back cover, revealing an author's small, boxed-in face seeming impossibly happy. I peel back the pages, disgruntled, as many of these texts tell an unrelatable narrative in my faith journey. Their chapters proclaim, as I do, that beauty comes from ash. Yet, their journey, their hope, seems as if the final page resolves all fear and finds a purpose in all things, through all things, producing a perfect believer. While they seem to have all the answers, my one big question remains: did this person ever know ash in the first place?

Do these gleaming writers know death and disease, grief and guttural sadness, shame, and fear that church will never feel like home again? Do flaws flitter in and out of their lives, like mine? Or do they own the perfect farmhouse with the handsome, five-o-clock-shadow husband to match? Have they reared stepping-stone, curly-haired kiddos who never melt down in the grocery store? Are all medical visits a perfect bill of health? I imagine they don't have bills with a family business like theirs, even zooming around in a bells-and-whistles suburban.

Following two or three nights of coercing myself to read four or five pages, I place the book on my bookshelf. Though I often jump to the conclusion, hoping to dodge the unrelatable tales while collecting a few words of life-altering wisdom, they seem to offer nothing more than "Jesus loves me. This I know." These authors forever rest in truths they find so easy to swallow, meeting their pillows with an airless conscience each night. Meanwhile, my nightmares aren't quite over. In their righteous heart-and-mind testimonies, I don't find Christ. Instead, all I walk away with is my looming bully, Comparison.

I can't have beauty without ash, as the other texts suggest. The first must follow the latter in this spiritual sequence, but it seems the embers of life's worst battles flicker forever for me, refusing to surrender as cinders. Divinity's threads are cut short by more and more of my blunders, outside fears, and internal woes that are as consistent as the North Star shining centerstage each night. Thus, beauty idles, holds back, and stays on reserve as I fight for my faith to feel real amid the muck of more and more reality.

Though this isn't true of all Christian literature, because my words will never compare to the convicting, bold, and honest works of C.S. Lewis, Charles Spurgeon, and the like, I confess that my bookmark rarely meets anything beyond chapter 3 in most modern Christian Living books. And with that unlovely note in mind, I thank you for reading this far, not for championing my story, but for discovering God championing yours.

Yes, this book shares countless rays of hope God has shone and continues to shine throughout my life, but I would be the full embodiment of a lie if I left you here to feel that my life is constant beams of sunlight. As I collected the last rays of light to fill these pages for you, the two months before I could breathe, "It's ready for the printing press," I visited the emergency room. I also had two ultrasounds and one CT scan, while a doctor scheduled a colonoscopy for me a few weeks later. Meanwhile, Josh's vehicle was totaled, and the engine in my car died two weeks after that. Daisy peed on our friends' new carpet, moving to more trivial yet tragic things, and Alfie tried to eat their dog. In addition, another three ultrasounds and three thousand dollars later, we are drowning in medical bills.

My wilderness can't pull off the facade of a frilly, joyous spring meadow. I can't allow these pages, myself, to remain untouched by life. I can't present myself as a woman who is never distracted by the world's lies. Alas, no, dear friend, I find myself in the same sandstorms, surrounded by endless cacti beds, tiptoeing through boulders of snakes and scorpions day in and day out. I, like you, fight lies at night, awake to days of doctors' appointments I dread, and force my way through afternoons of intrusive thoughts and mundane nothingness. I know death, know grief, know full well some gray patches of my life will never resolve to softer, more gracious hues until

I'm on streets paved with gold, looking into the eyes of a God whose love is so bright, so wondrous, I might never look away.

Instead of offering the keys to perfection, a spotless, fire-proof map from Miracle A to Miracle B, instant teleportation from slavery in Egypt to the Land of Milk and Honey, I offer you three of the balmiest, lovely, heavenly medicines to soften the heart and sharpen the faith. Like the medicine for my OCD, these truths won't poof away the tragedies, but they will dull the looming, pounding, negative thoughts and propose meaning instead.

With the first, I give you a kinder perception of God, reminding—no, challenging—you to believe in a God you can like. He is, indeed, mysterious and shows love in intense, sometimes incomprehensible, ways. Meanwhile, God is also wildly passionate, quirky by employing outcasts he wrangles to call friends, and sarcastic in the best of ways when addressing hypocritical Pharisees. This is a likable God you can laugh with over a cup of coffee. But best of all, his likability branches from a genuine, death-defying kindness.

Kindness puts up a humble but eruptive fight, offering the most vital blow against bitterness and deceit. However, to fully access this softer side of God's nature, you must first choose to look for it. That's not to say God's kindness doesn't permeate the world around us, but humans have mastered the ability to put down rose-colored glasses in exchange for a thorny pair of shades. Rarely do we settle in between the roses and thorns, being open to others yet guarding our hearts. Instead, all the bright, pretty petals catch our attention as we remain blind to the thorns, and after being pricked, feeling hurt, left out, and betrayed, we falsely assume all petals serve as deceivers.

Often, it only takes one human to break our trust, and as a means to protect ourselves, we label everyone else, including God, with our betrayer's worst characteristics. Tenuously, possibly unknowingly, we decorate our Savior with mankind's sinister tricks, hanging chains for garland, gray clouds as ornaments.

This "Pessimists Welcome" mentality creates hypersensitivity around security. *If you take off the thorny glasses, you'll be deceived again*, it whispers. *And again. And again.* It further warns: *make no room for other people's smiles, thoughtful gestures, or words of encouragement. Assume the worst and safe you shall be.*

But is safe genuinely safe if you remain inactive? How can an action verb, "to be safe," maintain its action without action? Hiding from people, relationships, and God isn't proactive. It's a wasteful, passive way to view others. It leaves no room for purpose, blocking out love and hope.

I'm not suggesting you sport rose-colored glasses. After all, they are just as deceptive, offering no room for discernment. Nonetheless, you might question: how can a small pair of thorny shades, meant to protect me, devastate all light and goodness? The moment we refuse someone's extension of love, we forget how to extend kindness to others. We too easily lend ourselves to breaking the cycle of goodness, thus becoming a contributing cause of the cyclic hurt and shame we see in the world, the sort of gloominess that we like to shift away from our reality. Meanwhile, we point our fingers at our big pile of ash, throw our faces toward heaven, and dare ask God why he won't allow the world a fair chance at good things.

Embrace the idea that God is kind. Give this thought a try. In this process, I guarantee that as you push yourself to believe in the goodness you can't see, you will embody the very thing you want God to be (the very thing he is). You will be the evidence, the tangible proof, of God's kindness. In this discovery, you will find yourself believing in God's goodness and choosing to be an active part of his command to love others more than yourself.

Second, rather than promise all life's hardest questions have answers on earth, I promise no season of this life lives without a glorious purpose.

On day one of my therapy, I was told OCD has no cure. There's no "happy pill," no "fix-all button," no hope that I'll wake up completely healed and whole while wearing this skin. Most scientists and psychologists only have a mere skeleton concept of OCD, limited knowledge. Yes, there is a proven problem in the communication of neurotransmitters between the frontal cortex and ventral striatum. Still, today's technology offers no additional steps and provides no solid, safe, and permanent solution to create healthy chemical balances in the brain.

Once my therapist revealed this heartache, I had two choices: wallow in the grief of a healed life that would never be mine or discover the purpose behind my earth-bound burden. I sat with the first choice for a while, allowing it to serve as a savage excuse for my bitterness, hatred, and pouting. It always felt good to relish my "deserved" pity, to simmer in something that wasn't my fault, until dodging the latter option was solely my fault. I had become a glutton for sympathy, yet I didn't want any help. The moment I received sound advice or a practical way to aid in my journey, I would have no excuse for my behavior.

I built so many barriers and seeped resentment into countless relationships, so I had no choice but to walk around my castle of isolation, praying if I persistently marched its four corners, the walls would come down. In this process of roaming through my worst nightmare, I learned that the walls slowly faded when I invited other people to know they weren't alone. When it was no longer about me and my grief but about promising others that life, despite OCD, has an enriching purpose. We are survivors because God knows our scars mean something eternal. Allowing others to see my honest journey with OCD and all its clunky baggage was a means of healing. It was a communal balm reminding me that God never leaves us on our own; he never means for hard times to devastate our worth. Instead, our brutal seasons serve as opportunities to scatter seeds in anticipation of the springtime, believing growth is God's plan for all of us.

Last, but necessary for all others to create harmony, I offer you hope, a bright light you can look to, even if it seems far in the distance. I know it's there. And in a broken world, a wilderness sick with sin and shame and hurt, there's little we know. Few tools we feel we can bank on to get us through hard times. But meanwhile, when we allow God to invite us into the unknown and welcome the most unimaginable, prickly people and places to have space in our lives, we find answers that don't always spell everything out but always satisfy our longing. When we love others, love—Love—becomes the only answer we need.

Regarding the Light, I must call you back to the story of Habakkuk. *Even If*'s Bible study so beautifully reveals: "[Habakkuk 3:4] portrays God as light. This is a common image used to describe the Lord in both the Old and New Testaments. In the context of the Exodus account, we are reminded of the shining glory of the Lord that was too holy and magnificent for Moses to even look upon. And yet our God who is light, and in whom is no darkness at all (1 John 1:5) has revealed himself to us, just as the unapproachable and magnificent light of God approaches us through Jesus."[1]

Christ is Light. Light and Christ are synonymous. If we have one, we have the other. Though we might feel unsure about what to do with such a bright, wonderous Light, let's recall other ways, more routine ways, we maximize light on earth:

We use our phone's flashlight to navigate a dark bedroom, dodging dirty clothes and dirtier dogs so we don't trip and hurt ourselves. We turn on the lantern when the storm surrounding our house destroys the

1. Schmucker, "Even If," para. 4

neighborhood's power, offering us a way to survive the tumultuous night. We strike a match to bring candles to life, offering a sweet, calming, simple light, a savor that fills our homes and hearts with glowing feelings of belonging.

Convenient enough, the reasons and ways we use light on earth perfectly parallel the purpose of God's light. I challenge you to let him be your one source of wisdom as twilight hides the sun. Allow God to help you navigate the dark. After all, he never intended for us to stumble and fall. Eden had a much kinder, brighter path in mind. Give God room to stay with you on endless nights when storms seem relentless. Make room for God to fill your home, your soul, with the sweetest sensation, a gentle, calming reminder that goodness, in his hands, is warmth.

These ideas are often hard to recognize because they appear as riddles with no reference. Yet, when you weather hard times and still choose God's goodness, you discover that the only answer you need is who he is. The only solution you need is Love. And between God and his Son's infinite display of love, exhaustion and exile find hope.

Only now have I displaced myself from the false illusion of a nostalgic Christianity to realize that here—in a day and time when dreams are still dreams robbed by present-day nightmares—love abounds. Love abides in a present-day hardship, diagnosis, fear, or wrong decision. Love remains relentless, not letting go while we wish for a better tomorrow.

Such unimaginable love is the Holy Spirit, the One residing with us down here, day in and day out, until Christ returns or says our time on earth is complete. Once we have traversed life's hardest lessons, we are welcomed to the dream, the happily ever after, the gates of heaven where the first thing God does isn't demand that we praise him, but instead, he honors us: "Well done, good and faithful servant!" (Matt 25:23). We can believe in the dream and hope because his love is undeniable in the present, despite our finite shortcomings and tragedies.

So, that is what this book is. It's a spine-and-pages glimmer of hope despite reality, a love cultivated by God that defies hopelessness, quiets chaos, and ensues an enteral purpose we can pursue forever on earth. And it is my honor, my soul's joy, to stand alongside you as our bellies ache with hunger, our throats long for water, our bodies yearn for solace and quiet. I find pride in standing beside you, even if our shoulders are hunched and you feel displaced from God and all good things. We can remind each other that we only know despair because hope exists, we only know longing because we know satisfaction wins, and we only know exhaustion because God gives us rest. Though these opposites are forever unable to stride synonymously, the weaker exists to juncture the stronger. The bad lays a purifying foundation for the good to settle forever in the soul.

You see, true success lives far beyond mere perfection. Rather, the success of a believer requires more grit, more heart, and more meaning besides doing things right for the sake of doing things right. As Christians, our success lies in accepting this: who we are isn't defined by our abilities but what we do with our incapability. We are defined by what we do with seasons, times, and failures that bring us to our knees, leave us wincing at our reflection, and force us to believe in God and goodness, not because we want to, but because there's no other place, no other warmth, worth calling our home. Survival offers gruesome nights but glorious mornings, getting to the other side of complicated things. It's a bittersweet exchange, but God never leaves us empty. Our wilderness has an end. And our soul wins as he welcomes us to a land free of lies, hurt, shame, and sin—for all eternity.

May you find his goodness amid all life has to offer. But on days when hope seems clouded by doubt, recall Jehovah Nissi, the Lord, our Banner. He goes before us, making way for his goodness to shine the path home.

> "But blessed is the one who trusts in the Lord, whose confidence is in him. They will be like a tree planted by the water that sends out its roots by the stream. It does not fear when heat comes; its leaves are always green. It has no worries in a year of drought and never fails to bear fruit." Jeremiah 17:7–8

Everyday Application:

1. Most of us have Christian books we've read (not including the Bible) that we don't like, don't agree with, could never get into, etc. However, think of a few Christian texts that have left you inspired. What about that text made you feel like you could further work on your relationship with God? Allow those texts to continue enriching your life, even after reading them.

2. Do you often find yourself embodying a "Pessimists Welcome" mentality? What seems to trigger these pessimistic mindsets? Is it a coworker? An in-law? What about someone who got what you wanted or seems to have their life together? In what ways can you choose to actively embody God's goodness and hope instead of feeding negativity?

3. Make a list of attributes of light. What does the sun offer? What can a flashlight do for you? After completing this list, see how those attributes parallel God as the Light.

4. Read Jeremiah 17:7–8 once more. Then again. Then again tomorrow. And on any other day in the future when the wilderness threatens your life and light, when you feel tired and hungry and halfway faithful. Until you truly believe God never leaves you in the drought, read it again.

Prayer Closet Thought:

If most of us are honest, the church has wounded us at least once. Regardless of your membership status, leadership role, or backseat, ten-minutes-late participation, none of us are shielded from the reality that church is a holy place that welcomes flawed humans to worship their Creator. Thus, a room filled with flawed people will leave a sad but undeniable space for hurt, confusion, anger, and frustration.

If you're like me, wary of most Christian literature, even most Christian churches' agendas, I encourage you to be honest with God about this struggle. Ask him to let you experience genuine love for Christ, a love so focused on him and others that a building filled with flawed people won't dictate whether or not you trust the Great I Am. Instead, you'll choose to trust him amid the imperfect people, amid the cheesy church texts, amid the days when Christians give each other bad reps. Allow Christ to curate a genuine heart deep in your bones. You will deter the enemy's obsession with forcing you to dodge any notion of Christian-ese culture.

Final Thoughts

✤

HUMANS RARELY ANTICIPATE THE sun each morning. It's an automated piece of nature serving as a heavy reminder that we must climb out of bed or else run late for work. We engulf its beauty in the chaos of routine. I must admit that I, too, neglected the miracle of each sunrise for years, groaning at the mere sight of the gold glimmer peeping through my bedroom blinds. However, after moving from Georgia to Colorado, my perception of sunlight shifted.

Each morning, I leash up my pups for a stroll, but before we reach the first stop sign on our routine trip, I've already looked for her, found her, noticed her, the sun. Back home, tall pine trees blocked her till midday. But here, in morning's wide-open skies, she boasts a soft yellow, a meek intensity the eyes can handle. Still, she quickly beckons you to shift your gaze and notice the cotton-candy sky: the baby pinks, baby blues, and lightest lavenders blanketing the world. Meanwhile, her sunlight reflects a glorious white light that bounces off the Rocky Mountains' snow-capped peaks, reminding you just how small you are in a holy, humbling way.

I search for the sun as a means of steadying my mind. It's an organic parallel to the Zoloft I down with my morning cup of coffee, which inclines me to believe that perhaps we don't need the bad to go away so long as the good is present. Maybe the beauty, though surrounded by ash, remains the miracle. After all, what would good be without bad? Could it be the hero if there was no villain to rescue us from? A healing balm apart from a stinging wound? A sun aside from storms?

Harriet Beecher Stowe, most known for her 19th-century novel *Uncle Tom's Cabin*, also wrote hymns—my favorite, *Still, Still with Thee*, inspired by her morning routine. Though such a practice is labeled dreaded and unwanted these days, she would wake up each morning at 4:30 to see the sunrise. Up before the roosters, she would "see the coming of the dawn, hear the singing of the birds, and . . . enjoy the overshadowing presence of her God."[1]

The four stanzas of *Still, Still with Thee* read:

> Still, still with thee, when purple morning breaketh,
> When the bird waketh, and the shadows flee;
> Fairer than morning, lovelier than daylight,
> Dawns the sweet consciousness, I am with thee.
>
> Alone with thee, amid the mystic shadows,
> The solemn hush of nature newly born;
> Alone with thee in breathless adoration,
> In the calm dew and freshness of the morn.
>
> When sinks the soul, subdued by toil, to slumber,
> Its closing eye looks up to thee in prayer;
> Sweet the repose beneath thy wings overshading,
> But sweeter still to wake and find thee there.
>
> So shall it be at last, in that bright morning,
> When the soul waketh and life's shadows flee;
> O in that hour, fairer than daylight dawning
> Shall rise the glorious thought: I am with thee!

I wonder if the children of Israel ever noticed—honestly noticed—the clouds, well, rather, the Cloud, the big, powerful Holy Spirit bellowing them onward, guiding them to a place of rest and peace promised to their forefather, Abraham, generations before. Despite their wanderings, ailments, and pure fatigue, they awoke each morning to a billowing Cloud that would never leave. A dependable promise bridging the gap from desolation to sheer delight.

The Bible hints that, at this time, the Holy Spirit was a roaring, "all-consuming fire" of a cloud, but perhaps what burned so bright was his passion for his children (Heb 12:29). Sure, my lack of presence amid their wilderness won't allow me to counteract the notion that the Holy Spirit offered a constant combustion of foxlike oranges and chili-pepper reds amid his billows. But I like to think his fire burned with the soft pinks, yellows,

---

1. Cobble Trantham, "Hymns," p. 46

and purples, the tender touch of color, decorating each morning. After all, that's when his grace is most fresh.

Tomorrow morning, I challenge you to look for the sun. Find her, notice her, and allow God to showcase his beaming love through her. Believe it or not, God's radiance, your sole hope, thrives amid the dry spaces and places filled with unexpected but everlasting milk and honey, the sweetest, purest kind.

Bibliography

Benedict, M. *The Other Einstein*. Sourcebooks Landmark. 2017.

Cobble Trantham, Cara. *Hymns*. 1. Vol. 1. Houston, TX: The Daily Grace Co., 2017.

Creation Studies Institute. (n.d.). *The complex system of the eye*. The Complex System of the Eye Retrieved April 28, 2022, from https://creationstudies.org/articles/who-is-god/272-complex-eye.

Female blacksmiths through history. Kama Bandsaws, Bandsaws from Elderfield & Hall. (2021, March 25). Retrieved May 4, 2022, from https://kamabandsaw.com/female-blacksmiths-through-history/

Ginter, Amber. "Jesus Knew Anxiety Too." iBelieve.com. Salem Web Media, December 21, 2021. https://www.ibelieve.com/health-beauty/jesus-knew-anxiety-too.html.

"History: D-Day: June 6, 1944: The United States Army." History | D-Day | June 6, 1944 | The United States Army. Accessed April 20, 2022. https://www.army.mil/d-day/history.html.

Morgan, Robert J. *Then Sings My Soul, Keepsake Edition*. Nashville, TN: Nelson Books, 2014.

Piper, Barnabas. "The Meaning of Jehovah Nissi and the Significance of God's Name for Today." biblestudytools.com. Salem Web Network, October 18, 2019. https://www.biblestudytools.com/bible-study/topical-studies/jehovah-nissi-the-lord-is-my-banner.html.

Schmucker, Kristin. *Even If*. Houston, Texas: The Daily Grace Co., 2017.

Shipley, John. "Miracle on Ice Special Coverage: How St. Paul's Herb Brooks and His Players Made History." Pioneer Press. MediaNews Group, February 19, 2020. https://www.twincities.com/2020/02/19/miracle-on-ice-40th-anniversary-team-usa-olympics/.

Swindoll, Chuck. "Habakkuk." Book of Habakkuk Overview - Insight for Living Ministries. Insight for Living Ministries. Accessed April 14, 2022. https://insight.org/resources/bible/the-minor-prophets/habakkuk.

"The Life & Times of Jesus of Nazareth: Did You Know?: Christian History Magazine." Christian History Institute, 1998. https://christianhistoryinstitute.org/magazine/article/life-and-times-of-jesus-did-you-know.

Wood, T. E. *The Engineer's Wife*. Sourcebooks Landmark. (2021)

Why is jeremiah called the weeping prophet? BibleAsk. (2022, March 17). Retrieved May 4, 2022, from https://bibleask.org/jeremiah-named-weeping-prophet/

You are here: Home. OCDUK. (n.d.). Retrieved May 5, 2022, from https://www.ocduk.org/ocd/world-health-organisation/